C000083613

CHRISTMAS

A collection of poetry about Christmas,
from poets around the world.

Compiled by ROBIN BARRATT

Published by THE POET

THE POET

A leading international online poetry magazine, recognized for both its quarterly themed collections, and its interviews with poets worldwide; looking at their work and their words, and what motivates and inspires them to write.

Interviews, profiles, articles, quarterly collections, Poet of the Week and Young Poets.

W: www.ThePoetMagazine.org
E: Robin@ThePoetMagazine.org

~

CHRISTMAS
A collection of poetry about Christmas,
from poets around the world.

Published by THE POET

ISBN: 9798564859837

Cover image and design: Canva
www.Canva.com

THANK YOU!

THANK YOU TO EVERYONE, EVERYWHERE SUPPORTING THE POET; WITHOUT YOUR HELP WE WOULDN'T BE ABLE TO CONTINUE SHOWCASING INSPIRING POETS AND PUBLISHING AMAZING POETRY FROM AROUND THE WORLD...

...AND WHAT A DULL WORLD THAT WOULD BE!

You can support us too by buying a copy of our collections, donating, or even sponsoring us. We are a not-for-profit, so everything goes back into developing and promoting the website, publishing our quarterly collections and interviewing and profiling poets worldwide.

Go to the website for further details:

www.ThePoetMagazine.org

OTHER COLLECTIONS FROM THE POET

A NEW WORLD - Rethinking our lives post-pandemic.
Sixty seven poets from around the world all writing on the theme of A NEW WORLD; exploring life post-pandemic.
115 poems/225 pages
ISBN: 9798696477084

SUMMER 2020 – ON THE ROAD Volumes 1 & 2
With one hundred and twenty poets from around the world, ON THE ROAD, is probably one of the largest international anthologies of travel poetry ever published.
Vol.1: 135 poems / 240 pages
ISBN: 9798640673593
Vol. 2: 117 poems / 245 pages
ISBN: 9798665956312

SPRING 2020 – WAR & BATTLE
Fifty-four poets from around the world all writing on the theme of WAR & BATTLE.
103 poems/215 pages.
ISBN: 9798629604594

WINTER 2019 - THE SEASONS
Thirty-four poets from around the world all writing on the theme of THE SEASONS.
80 poems/129 pages.
ISBN: 9798600084445

AUTUMN 2019 - LOVE
Twenty-nine poets from around the world all writing on the theme of LOVE.
73 poems/119 pages.
ISBN: 9781699169612

NEW - POETRY WRITING COURSE

Covering both contemporary free verse, and the more traditional poem, THE POET'S Poetry Writing course takes you through the elements that make amazing poetry, and the skills, methods and techniques that you can use to begin exploring poetry for the first time, or to help develop and better your own work.

MODULES INCLUDE:

- A brief history of poetry.
- The Poetic Audience.
- Genres and Themes.
- Meaning and Form.
- Form and Structure.
- Using Form to enhance impact.
- Metaphor, Simile and Figurative language.
- Metre and Rhythm.
- Free Verse.
- Rhyming Verse.
- Using punctuation.
- Defining your voice.
- Experimental Techniques.
- How and where to publish.
- Publishing your book, Commercial Publishing and self-publishing.

For further information and to download the course, go to:

www.thepoetmagazine.org

and click on **Poetry Writing Course**.

CONTENTS

Page

119. Bill Cushing - USA
123. Jyotirmaya Thakur - ENGLAND / INDIA
127. Bozena Helena Mazur-Nowak - ENGLAND / POLAND
131. Eleni Vasileiou-Asteroskoni - GREECE / GERMANY
133. Seher Hashmi - KINGDOM OF BAHRAIN
137. David Dephy - USA / GEORGIA
141. Emily Braddock - ENGLAND
143. Jill Clark - USA
145. Mark Fleisher - USA
149. Sarah James - ENGLAND
151. Judy DeCroce - USA
153. Antoni Ooto - USA
155. Tracy Davidson - ENGLAND
159. Máire Malone - ENGLAND / REPUBLIC OF IRELAND
161. Nivedita Karthik - INDIA
163. Russell Willis - USA
167. Laurinda Lind - USA
169. Deepika Singh - INDIA
171. Anthony Ward - ENGLAND
173. Dr. Sarah Clark - KINGDOM OF BAHRAIN
177. John Tunaley - ENGLAND
179. Gerri Leen - USA
183. Margaret Clifford - AUSTRALIA
185. Cathy Cade - ENGLAND
189. Bernadette Perez - USA
191. Hussein Habasch - KURDISTAN / GERMANY
193. Lovelle Sumayang - PHILIPPINES
195. William Khalipwina Mpina - MALAWI
199. Stella Peg Carruthers - NEW ZEALAND
203. John Grey - USA / AUSTRALIA
205. Peter H. Dietrich - BULGARIA / UK
209. Yash Seyedbagheri - USA
211. Eva Petropoulou-Lianoy - GREECE
215. Mike Wilson - USA
217. Eduard Schmidt-Zorner - REPUBLIC OF IRELAND / GERMANY
221. Ndaba Sibanda - ZIMBABWE / ETHIOPIA
223. Francis H. Powell - ENGLAND
225. Kathryn Sadakierski - USA
229. Utpal Chakraborty - INDIA
233. LindaAnn LoSchiavo - USA
235. Dr. Archana Bahadur Zutshi - INDIA
237. Mantz Yorke - ENGLAND
239. Mark Andrew Heathcote - ENGLAND
241. Lou Faber - USA
243. Dr. Eftichia Kapardeli - GREECE
245. David A Banks - ENGLAND

247. Martin Chrispine Juwa – MALAWI
249. Maliha Hassan – PAKISTAN
253. Donna Zephrine – USA
255. Alicja Maria Kuberska – POLAND
257. Lindsay Ronald - CANADA
259. June G Paul - USA
261. Keith Burton – USA
263. Gabriella Garofalo - ITALY
265. Wilda Morris – USA
269. Veda Varma - KINGDOM OF BAHRAIN
273. Mary Anne Zammit – MALTA
275. Ed Ruzicka – USA

CHRISTMAS

A collection of poetry about Christmas,
from poets around the world.

Charlotte Langtree
ENGLAND

Charlotte is an author and poet from the North-West of England. Her work has been published by the *Inner Circle Writers' Magazine* and *WPC Press*, and is due to be featured in upcoming anthologies by Eerie River Publishing, Black Hare Press, Iron Faerie Publishing, and Paper Djinn Press.
E: c-d-b@hotmail.co.uk
W: www.charlottelangtree.wordpress.com

THE GIFT OF CHRISTMAS

The ruby burn of mulled wine
Down my throat,
And the mismatch of homemade baubles
On the tree;
This means Christmas to me.
I spend this time
Soaking in the festive blend
Of gingerbread and cheerful cards
From old friends,
Listening to sing-along songs
My parents danced to
Way back when.
And the sweetest gift,
The one that lifts
My heart
And outshines
The tinsel gold and silver bells,
Is the gift of love
And time, no longer apart
But together
In flesh and spirit, and mind,
Cherishing
Warm hugs and wide smiles,
'Neath the mistletoe kissing.
And remembering
The ones we're missing.

WINTER'S MAGIC

There's something about
The darkness of nights
Glittered with the frosted flakes
Of first snow,
Alight
With the ice of cold-burning stars,
Christmas lights aglow
Like bright fireflies in shining jars.
Warm breath mists the air,
A sign of life in the dark,
As sweet-sung carols
Dance and drift
Through sky and hearts.
Wrapped up, cosy and snug,
In hats and gloves
And woollen scarves,
The taste of Winter's magic
On the tongue;
The spirit of Christmas is strong.

Jim Landwehr
USA

Jim has published five poetry collections; *Thoughts From A Line At The DMV, Written Life, Reciting From Memory, On A Road* and *Genetically Speaking*. He also has three published memoirs, *Cretin Boy, The Portland House: A 70's Memoir* and *Dirty Shirt: A Boundary Waters Memoir*. He has non-fiction stories published in *StoryNews, Main Street Rag* and others. His poetry has been featured in *Torrid Literature Journal, Blue Heron Review, Off the Coast Poetry Journal,* and many others. Jim served as the 2018-2019 poet laureate for the Village of Wales, Wisconsin.
E: jimlandwehr@att.net
W: www.jimlandwehr.com

THE VISITOR

If the ghost of my Christmas past
paid me a visit
what would I see?
I'd see ribbon candy and mixed nuts
in a living room buzzing with relatives.
I'd smell rib roast and potatoes
beneath a haze of cigarette smoke.
I'd taste pumpkin pie with cool whip
and egg nog from a dainty glass.
I'd hear shouts of
"Thank you, Mom!"
"It's perfect!"
"Save the bows!"
And I'd feel like I was enveloped in love,
safe and warm
like I never wanted the night to end

If the ghost of Christmas present
paid me a visit
what would I see?
I'd see my two twenty-something kids
in their pyjamas on Christmas morning
I'd smell coffee and ebelskivers
and the scent of evergreen.
I'd taste the marshmallow and fruit
of our chocolate fondue tradition.
I'd hear carols seeping from the stereo
Bing, and Perry and Nat King Cole.
And I'd still feel enveloped in love,
grateful and fortunate
like my heart was given a great gift.

If the ghost of Christmas future
paid me a visit
what would I see?
I'd see that family always comes first
I'd breathe in the redemption in Christ's birth
I'd taste the sweetness of a life well lived
I'd hear the call to be present and love big
and I'd feel like I'd lived a beautiful dream.

Linda Imbler

USA

Linda is the author of three poetry collections published by Amazon. Soma Publishing has also published three of her poetry books; *Pairings* (a hybrid of short fiction and poetry), *The Sea's Secret Song,* and *That Fifth Element*. Since writing her first poem five years ago, her poetry and short stories have appeared both locally and internationally. In addition to putting pen and paper to inventive use, Linda is an avid reader and budding illustrator. This writer, yoga practitioner, and classical guitar player lives in Wichita, Kansas with her husband, Mike the Luthier, several quite intelligent saltwater fish, and an ever-growing family of gorgeous guitars. She has been nominated for a Pushcart Prize and several Best of the Nets.

E: mike-imbler@cox.net

Blog: www.lindaspoetryblog.blogspot.com

BELLS AND BERRIES
Within the Nativity

Bloomed cactus and rose, don fancy Yule clothes
Joseph, Mary, Jesus

Piled Yule log blocks, a bright Christmas box
Adoration, Celebration, Decoration

Greeting cards and cakes, sweet fruit pies to bake
wooden barrels, water troughs, crooks

Clear carols and cheer, for loved ones so dear
Caspar, Melchoir, Balthazar

Crisp cookies and crackers, for midnight snackers
donkeys, oxen, lambs

Warm pudding and presents, holiday music events
gold, frankincense, myrrh

Ornaments on trees, shelled chestnuts and wreaths
Michael, Olivia, Angel Unknown

Sliced turkey and ham, add nice figgy jam
fisherman, shepherds, bakers

Stockings and stars, all these things are:

Offered to you in the hopes you will find the peace, joy and comfort
we all seek during this special time of the year.

UNDER THE TREE

Under the tree
on Christmas Day,
toys and games,
fun, fantastic things
for a small boy.

What he wants above all else though,
no one can give him,
his beloved grandma's presence.
This will not come about.
She is passed into another realm
and cannot visit.

What use are toys and play things
to a lonely child
whose only desire is to be reunited
with the one whom he loved the best?
What cure for sadness, melancholy
when the meaning of death
is also beyond the understanding
of those who profess adulthood?

Children talk during funerals,
asking about the deceased.
They walk over graves,
with no realization.
They ask and they wait
for returns that will never happen.
For surely,
a mistake is been made,
and children believe
adults can set things to right.

Time will soften the edges of pain,
a permanent dull ache replacing.
But for now,
children learn to ask
for what they are expected to ask for,
toys and games,
not for what they may really be wishing
was sitting under the tree.

Lorraine Caputo
ECUADOR / USA

Lorraine is a documentary poet, translator and travel writer. Her works appear in over 180 journals on six continents, such as *Prairie Schooner* (US), *Revista Máquina Combinatoria* (Ecuador), *übergang* (Germany), *Open Road Review* (India), Cordite Poetry Review (Australia) and Bakwa (Cameroon); and 12 chapbooks of poetry – including *Caribbean Nights* (Red Bird Chapbooks, 2014), *Notes from the Patagonia* (dancing girl press, 2017) and *On Galápagos Shores* (dancing girl press, 2019). She also pens travel pieces, with stories appearing in the anthologies *Drive: Women's True Stories from the Open Road* (Seal Press, 2002) and *Far Flung and Foreign* (Lowestoft Chronicle Press, 2012), and travel articles and guidebooks. In March 2011, the Parliamentary Poet Laureate of Canada honoured her verse. She has done over 200 literary readings, from Alaska to the Patagonia. Originally from North America, Ms Caputo has been journeying through Latin America for the past three decades, listening to the voices of the pueblos and Earth. During the pandemic, she has been observing life in the equatorial Andes.
E: lazafada@hotmail.com
FB:@lorrainecaputo.wanderer
Blog: @latinamericawanderer.wordpress.com

MÉRIDA MAGI

In the oldest cathedral
                    on the American continent
            built of Maya temple stones
On the day the Three Kings
            visited the manger
                    in this side chapel

Mary tenderly places the Christ child in his cradle
Joseph presents him with an out-stretched hand
Slowly the Magi approach
            passing by a giant cow
                    by a giant tapir
Yellow lights drape the plastic pine boughs
            & dried palm fronds hung
                    with colourful glass ornaments
They wink in electronic rhythm to

Oh, All ye faithful coming
            shepherds   magi   & others
Hark! Do you hear the herald angels singing
            with the jingling bells?
Even Santa Claus is coming to this town
            on this silent night
                    when joy has entered the world
Frosty the Snowman watches
            those who come a-wassailing

            Through the open windows
                    wrought-iron-grilled
                the sound & smell of traffic passes
            The chapel begins to resound
                with the cathedral bells pealing
                        for five-o-clock mass

NATIVITY

Near midnight on Christmas Eve
Within the aged church
A line of people slowly passes to the front

Each stoops to kiss
the Christ child nestled
in the arms of a woman
A nun stands next to her
handkerchief in hand
ready to wipe away lipstick

Fathers with their young sons and daughters
stop in front of the manger
framed in winking lights
to ponder the miracle
of the still-empty cradle

After the last mother, the last child
has welcomed that baby
He is laid into the straw-bedded cradle
his hands wide open to this world
his fat legs kicking the air

& the families step into the streets
washed clean by the rain
the sunset lightning had forebode

SOUNDS OF SILENCE

These Christmas Eve streets
echo with the mournful
song of a blind
man's accordion

These Christmas Eve streets
beneath the dim light
of a waning crescent moon
yet to be arisen

These Christmas Eve streets
echoing with the footfall
of families going to mass

announced by silent bells
the cry of a new-born
babe in a manger

in a parish church
bathed in the perfume
of *palo santo*

The silence of footfalls
upon centuries-old
wooden floors

the silence of prayers
before the crèche broken
by a baby's cry

These Christmas Eve streets
echoing with the silence
of the departed blind
accordion

Mirela Salkovic Hadzic
BOSNIA & HERZEGOVINA / CROATIA

Mirela is a Croatian freelance journalist and poet living in Tuzla. An activist for human rights, she has had three books published in Croatia; two of poetry and the third, stories for children.
E: mirela.mery@hotmail.com
FB: @MirelaReaHadzic
Blog: @MirelinBlog
Blog: @ReinaKuhinja

MERRY CHRISTMAS

Hey dear...

Christmas is coming,
our favourite days,
when we share joy.
Do you remember,
the last one,
when you sang,
with the turkey,
and made jokes,
with the postman,
that one,
who brought you,
a cat, as my gift.
Let we reunite,
this year too,
and cherish the love,
that God gave us,
let's make punch, again,
and dance waltz,
with me,
while we are drunk.

Oh, Christmas is coming,
my darling,
Santa have prepared,
his gifts, be sure,
that I Will tell him,
you was a good man.
Just, be sure.
Christmas is almost here.
Let's pray my love.
And hope, that everyone,
Will be safe and loved.
Let's pray for homeless,
that they find a warm place,
a lovely home.
Let God send joy and happiness
to all people.
Let this Christmas,
we feel more love,
then we felt,

the last one.
Do you know,
Christmas is coming,
it's time for joy.
Have you decorated
your tree, with pretty angels?
I did.
I made these days,
a lots of food,
to share with orphaned kids,
that they feel happiness,
on this time of year.
Have I told you lately,
I went in church,
to light up candles,
for your health and joy.
I have prayed for you,
since I dreamed of you,
last night.
I just want you to know,
am thinking about you a lot,
and wish you to spend,
a cheerful and the best
Christmas ever.
I Will send you a cookies,
that I've made,
and a letter,
with pictures of mine,
with my cats,
and my parents,
while we baked a cake.
I hope that everything
is fine, at you.
P.S. I love you.

Good morning,
beautiful people.
Christmas is coming.
Can you feel the love,
and joy, that's coming
to us?
Can we hug someone,
and share the happiness,
around us?
Let's spread love,
and sing together with me.

Let's pray.
Let's hope.
Let's love each others.
Let's do a good things.
Let's forgiving each others.
Because, we are one.
We are all family.
Merry Christmas to all.

Joan Mcnerney
USA

Joan's poetry is found in many literary magazines such as *Seven Circle Press, Dinner with the Muse, Poet Warriors, Blueline*, and *Halcyon Days*. Four Bright Hills Press Anthologies, several *Poppy Road* Journals, and numerous *Poets' Espresso Reviews* have also accepted her work. She has four Best of the Net nominations. Her latest title is *The Muse in Miniature*.
E: poetryjoan@statetel.com

TWELVE STEPS TO WINTER

1   Kicking up piles of foliage,
the wind tries to enter my house.

2   I can see my breath right
in front of me now.

3   Maple leaves, oak leaves, all fall
leaves tumbling through air.

4   Window panes clattering like
nervous teeth at midnight.

5   Frost pinches my cheeks, kissing me.
A cool, cruel lover.

6   Quickly, quietly needles of snow
embroider tall fir trees.

7   That must be my friends stamping
their boots outside.

8   As the kettle boils, aromas of hot
cider spice the kitchen.

9   Our favourite songs stream
through hallways.

10   Sparkling butter cookies melting
in our mouths.

11   A tiger cat with big green eyes
tosses balls of yarn.

12   Galaxies of snow stars whirling
every which way.

ANGEL

I want to make an angel
in the snow though I am
old for that sort of thing.

That is something I have
never done. A woman from
Vermont told me about it.

Nobody made slush angels
in Brooklyn...unheard of...
with no meadows to angel in.

We just threw hard packed
snowballs at each other
sliding over icy streets.

Now I will take my pick
of snow. Find a perfect
field of that lush white stuff.

I will lay down on a cool bed
flapping my arms up and down
to make sacred patterns.

Yes, I will angel away
over and over until finally
I fly off to heaven.

Want to wing it with me?

ARCTIC FLURRIES

Winds toss foliage in air.
Birds bend against frost
their wings catching the
last sunlight.

In cosmic dance snowflakes
light up evening.
Diminutive
galaxies circling abandoned gardens.

We hunch our shoulders with winter.
Our shadows are long now.

Finola Scott
SCOTLAND

Finola's poems are found on posters, tapestries and postcards They are published and anthologised widely in the UK & Eire, as well as internationally in the USA & Mexico. Publications included *New Writing Scotland, The Fenland Reed, PB, Orbis and Lighthouse*. Red Squirrel Press publish her pamphlet *Much left Unsaid*. She is currently Makar of the Federation of Writers (Scotland). She enjoys performing, and has read at many events and festivals; highlights include in the Scottish Parliament, The Edinburgh Book Festival, St Giles Cathedral and Rosslyn Chapel by candlelight.
E: Finolascott@yahoo.com
FB: @FinolaScottPoems

NIGHT WATCH
Haymarket Station, Edinburgh.

It's past eleven on Christmas Eve
and I'm swaddled in the echoing station.
You call & text all day with
staccato bulletins of weather & delays:
frozen rails, pointless
grey lakes and hills blinded by blizzards.
Migrating fieldfares blown off-course.

Now I'm here and
nearly you.
Arrival boards flash happy as tinsel,
trains glide into the Castle's lea,
no Santa Expresses but eager diesels.

Suddenly you're there.
Striding tall, you wave semaphore, heft your bag.
Scarlet scarf, gloves - gift wrapped for Scotland,
Then you're in my arms.
My winter visitor, on course.

Version published in *Dreich* magazine, Dec '20.

TOGETHER FOR CHRISTMAS

Outside dark drapes, stars gleam
meteors swirl as the Aurora dances.
Cosseted salads thrive in greenhouses.
Safely deep, bulbs ripen, daffodils dream
of swaying in Spring's sweet gardens.

Inside, round the candle-bright table
faces freed from photo-frames glow.
Grannies grin, finish anecdotes and toast
their tinselled broods. Crystal winks,
crackers crack as potatoes are speared.
Party-hatted, tucked in tight, our future
chuckles from her high chair.

Kabishev Alexander Konstantinovich

RUSSIA

Kabishev is a student, aspiring poet and writer, founder and head of the international creative and cultural project DEMO GOG, and editor-in-chief of the student newspaper *DEMO GOG*.
E: aleksandar.kabishev@yandex.ru

WHAT IS CHRISTMAS?
Translation from Russian by Lovelle Sumayang

What is Christmas?
Tell me please!
Just way happy
To increase?

What is Christmas?
I want know!
Is it season
Full of snow?

What is Christmas
For you friend?
This is something
Never end!

What is Christmas?
We all know
Play important
For us role!

MAGIC BALL
Translation from Russian by Lovelle Sumayang

Crystal ball with snow inside,
Cherished dreams get revived
Shake it once, behold in stride -
Snowstorms whirled light in jive.

It's like the whole world is in it,
Its bustle is covered by glass of it,
And every day is like new genesis,
Promising a lot of worries.

But in it, the water will dissipate,
The next event, who can anticipate?
Then, what can't be recovered,
Memories can be restored!

NEW YEAR
Translation from Russian by Lovelle Sumayang

Now the arrow is at the timer,
Piercing the time's cover,
Eager to complete its perimeter,
As if by chance, sudden or quicker.

No doubt, it was not an easy year,
But it went around the bend,
And something new then,
Time has brought us by the river.

The past, everyday, they linger,
Even shadow of sorrow, we'll remember,
We'll take best with us, not just better,
And we will carry it into the future.

There is music in the new year,
Like a highway leads to fate in there,
And who will hear and go further?
That will find in itself, the new year.

Julia Carlson
USA

Julia is a Bostonian, a graduate of Boston University and *diplomée* from the University of Toulouse le Mirail (France). She is the author of *Prayer for the Misbegotten* (Oddball Press, 2017) and *Little Creatures* (Wilderness House Press, 2019). Her poems have appeared in *Muddy River. Poetry Review, Nixes Mate Review, Ibbetson Street, Lyrical Somerville*, and others. She served as Fiction Editor of the *Wilderness House Literary Review*, and editor of *Bagel Bards Anthology V*. She has been surviving the pandemic by gardening, reading, and a wee dram at sunset or on a cold night.
E: gagecarlson@gmail.com
Instagram: @Uberhuss

CHRISTMAS CARD FROM CHARLOTTE

Charlotte's proud to tell you
just how old she is
what she likes and doesn't.
She starts work on her Christmas cards in July
so she'll have enough time to pick
the right card for the right person
"Very important" she says.
Mine arrives just after Thanksgiving
the envelope smothered in scotch tape
a nativity drawn inside a Christmas ball
with two sheep watching over
Baby Jesus asleep in a straw crib.
I like this tranquil scene she chose for me
In her hard-to-define way
she knows I need peace as much as
she needs to send it to me.

First published in *Little Creatures*, Wilderness House Press, 2019.

Shabbirhusein K. Jamnagerwalla
TANZANIA

Shabbirhusein is based in Dar es Salaam. He has been writing poetry for the past fifty years, and has had is work published number of local, national and international publications. On top of this, his poem *Dancing into our Lives* was featured in Chaotic *Times: Poetry Vaccine for Covid 19* by Brenda Mohamed and Florabell Lutchman, and he has been honoured during India's 74th Independence by the Motivational Strips & India's Literary Forum, Gujarat Sahitya Academy, and awarded the Kairat Duissenov Medal For Poetic Excellence for his poem *Kairat, You Are Missed!*
E: sitaronkajaan@gmail.com

CHRISTMAS IN 2020

Christmas is usually a time to be merry
Enjoy with family and friends
Indulge in happy occasions
Frolic in robust celebrations
Share your lovely gifts with all
And help to bring some happiness to the helpless.

Yet come 2020 on the calender
And some people have forgotten happiness
And others have immense difficulties
The World's economies have collapsed
Some of the restaurants and pubs are on curfews
The malls and markets are empty
People are moving around the cities
Wearing masks and with sanitizers handy
No hugging and no handshakes
No giveaways from Santa Clause
Parties are cancelled too
Social distancing is everywhere.
The spark of Christmas time has diminished.

Oh what a shame!
Covid 19 has rocked our world drastically
Careful brother and sister
We still have to swim strenuously
And guard ourselves
From the perils of Covid 19!
Whatever the true facts
Wishing all my friends
A Christmas full of happiness and joy!

Maxine Rose Munro
SCOTLAND

Maxine is a Shetlander adrift on the outskirts of Glasgow. After spending the first eighteen years of her life exclusively on the islands, without even a small break for the holidays, the culture shock experienced on eventually seeing the wider world rocked her to the core, and is still rocking now. However, as the end result appears to be poetry, she's fairly OK with this. Her poetry has been widely published, exhibited at a poetry festival, even won some prizes occasionally. She runs First Steps in Poetry feedback programme, which offers beginner poets free feedback and support.
E: maxinerosemunro@gmx.co.uk
W: www.maxinerosemunro.com
FB: @maxinerosemunro
Twitter: @MaxineRoseMunro

CHRISTMAS EVE GUISING

Dad brought back the masks
he'd bought in the toy shop in town,
and we'd squabble over
who had what – the duck, the wolf,
the cat.

Then, bundled in clothes stolen
from every wardrobe, we'd head out
into the night, troop about
the countryside, calling
at doors.

At every house the same game,
ways to weasel out our names
(though they never did), and then
they gave us coins, cordial, some
seed cake.

And so on, and on, and on,
in the dark, always stars above,
always snow on the ground,
in every house a tree lit bright, silver
with tinsel.

I never did see that they knew
our names, I never caught their winks.
All I saw was through the eyes
of a mask, and it showed me nothing
but magic.

NOTE: It was still traditional for young children to go guising on Christmas Eve when I was growing up in the Shetland Isles. Sadly, this tradition has now died out, replaced by trick or treating at Halloween.

NE'ER DAY MORNING

This morning everyone sleeps, but me.
This new morning that is a new year,
and everyone in this house sleeps
but me,

I inhale air no different to yesterday,
nor yesterday's yesterday. Everything
is the same – baubles and lights,
as before,

adorn a plastic tree I switch on by myself,
and look at by myself, this New Year
same-everything morning that I
don't sleep

and they do. I listen to the quiet that comes
before noise as calm before storms.
Soon they'll rise, full of alive,
sweep me

up in their wake, unresisting, until
I'm beached once more on some
peaceful shore, as now,
a voyeur

of mine own, cocooned in their wildness
that's my stability. This new morning
new year in which everything is still
the same,

I am glad.

NOTE: From 1583 Scottish people celebrating Christmas could be excommunicated, and though this was repealed in 1712 the Church continued to frown upon festive celebrations. Punishments for celebrating Yule were harsh, and there was no public holiday for the Scottish people on Christmas Day until 1958, meaning that the Scots would focus their celebrations on New Year's Eve (Hogmanay) and the day after (Ne'er Day).

Ne'er day morning was first published in nine muses poetry.

A PERFECT CHRISTMAS

Christmas music, Christmas food, Christmas lights,
and you.
A present mountain under a tree, merry, jolly,
and you.
A Christmas Carol on telly, mistletoe and holly,
you.
Snow if it's there, rain's more likely, still there's
you.
Angels with shepherds, Santa in his sleigh,
always there is you.
A Christmas of all things lovelier than the last,
none ever so perfect as you.

Rita B. Rose
USA

Rita is an award winning Italian-American poet living in West Babylon, New York. She is also internationally published. Her books include, *the exposé, Asylum: from the inside, Veranda Sundown, twisted poetry and prose*, and her newest poetry collection is *Flower Poems: Personalities in Bloom*. Christmas is her favourite holiday and she believes in keeping the spirit, year round.
E: Stonewallrusty@aol.com

SANTA SONNET

He comes in the wee of Christmas morning
when all are asleep and counting their sheep
across rooftops and lawns; jangling Buckhorns
frolicking and taking one final leap

And with a *HO HO HO* leading the way
his beard of white and cap of red and green
Santa Claus rides on his magical sleigh
talking to reindeer in language of neigh

Balancing atop chimneys; they do stop
helping Kris bring gifts to good girls and boys
and stuffing so many colourful socks
a token of love; sweets, clothing and toys

Spreading love and joy he is on his way
vowing to return one more Christmas day

Tamar Smith
SCOTLAND

Tamar is 10 years-old and lives in Glasgow. She loves to write stories and poems, and has already had a poem published in a national anthology. She LOVES Christmas, and has a birthday at Christmas too.

CHRISTMAS

Christmas, a time for family,
   decorations on the shelves
Over there, a Christmas tree,
   and here a door for elves.

Christmas is a time of year,
   you hope for all year round.
Elves use their Christmas magic here,
   So Santa won't be found.

Getting all the presents done,
   Gives Santa's mood a lift.
The children will not have much fun,
   If they don't get their gifts.

Elves pranks and tricks annoy you
   There's glitter everywhere!
They can't help but surprise you,
   And make you stop and stare.

Christmas, a time for family,
   Decorations on the shelves.
Over there, a Christmas tree,
   And here, a door for elves.

Ella Nathanael Alkiewicz
USA

Ella is a Labrador Inuk poet, writer and digital artist. She has been published in *Attack Bear Press* and in the anthology *Locating Me, Lucky Jefferson*. Ella lives in Massachusetts with her family and misses her relatives across North America.
E: ella.alkiewicz@gmail.com
Instagram: IG: @ella_alk
Twitter: @ellaalk

CHRISTMAS EVE

My Inuit relatives attend a magnanimous church service -
Kuve Inovia!

Their services last for hours across days,
The services for the pious and the peaceful and the lost.
Candles set in apples, an organ swells,
Hymnals, old wooden pews, Moravian stars.

> Voices sing in tune
> Voices of the elders
> Voices sing off-key
> Voices of suguset

My American relatives attended the Protestant service -
Merry Christmas!

The Church on the Village Green full of the *Who's Who* in town,
Their services made me fidget & giggle, whisper!
Candles in a paper holder, an organ bellows,
Hymnals, cushioned pews, garland.

> Voices sang in tune
> Voices of the elderly
> Voices heard off-key
> Children voices

My blended family of three forego the church services -
Happy Holidays!

The 1988 movie *Die Hard* plays while the tree lights dance upon the ceiling.
The presents under the tree and the posik eats the bows.
No candles in apples, no organ muzak booming,
No books, no bony butt pews, no wafting aromas.

> The giggles of my family are melodic
> The words my Angutik speaks with conviction
> The stories told by our panik fills me with pride
> The voices of my kin are the best-ever

Kuve Inovia! Merry Christmas!

Amrita Valan
INDIA

Amrita holds a master's degree in English literature, and has worked in several Business process outsourcing companies, as well as in American health and British motor insurance. She has also worked as a content creator (Deductive Logic and Reasoning in English-simulated questions for MBA Aspirants), and a receptionist at a five-star hotel. Amrita has written over a thousand poems on Love, Spirituality, Family, Religion, Current Affairs, Human Rights, short stories, rhymes and tales for children, and has just started exploring the thrill of trying to become a published poet.
E: amritavalan@gmail.com

PREPARING FOR CHRISTMAS

My mother put me in charge of the lights
I played with the twinkly bulbs red, blue, lilac and green, so bright!
I coiled it around my little tree,
With snowflakes of cotton wool made by me.
I wondered about the boxes up in the topmost shelf,
Had Santa left them early? Was it his elf?

From the kitchen came aroma of cinnamon buns,
Laced with ginger and honey and loads of fun
I loved the crisp apple crumble only mamma could make
Now she called me to the kitchen, aha! tastings to take!

It's just a day away! Christmas Eve my fairy gay!
Oh where shall I place my red stocking?
We don't have fireplaces in India,
Mom suggests I hook it up behind the doorway!

And so it's Christmas Eve
And a lovely dinner's been had,
My heart feels grateful my tummy feels glad.
Mamma, Papa and I, for Jesus, a candle we light
Read from the Bible, say prayers at midnight.

A huge slice of gooey chocolate cake, topped with nuts,
Then off to bed, as mamma won't listen to my buts.
It is sweet goodnight folks,
For Christmas follows tomorrow,
Dispelling all meanness, all anger, all sorrows!

CAROLLING AWAY!

Elgin road busy at the break of morning,
From our penthouse apartment,
I look down on canvas awnings
Of coffee shops and restaurants
Selling breakfast fare
Bright red suited bands of Santas,
Carolling away without a care.

I know we are up too high
For them to come to our door,
I race down in the lift, in
My nightgown and pina-fore!

Singing Joy to the World and
Jingle Bells with the lads,
Aah! Now that's indeed
A merry Christmas to be had!

Paul A. Freeman
UNITED ARAB EMIRATES

Paul is the author of *Rumours of Ophir*, a crime novel which was taught at 'O' level in Zimbabwean high schools and has been translated into German. In addition to having two novels, a children's book and an 18,000-word narrative poem commercially published (*Robin Hood and Friar Tuck: Zombie Killers!*), Paul is the author of hundreds of published short stories, poems and articles.
E: apaulfreeman@yahoo.co.uk
W: www.paulfreeman.weebly.com

RUDOLPH THE RED-NOSED REINDEER

Poor Rudolph was a reindeer with a nose
resembling a bulb of bright red hue.
The other reindeer laughed and said, "It glows
like Santa's after knocking back a few."
They called him 'Scarlet Schnozz' and wouldn't play
or socialise with Rudolph till a mist
descended on the eve of Christmas Day
and threatened every young child's Yuletide list.
Then Santa noticed Rudolph's nasal light,
and said to him, "There's naught for us to fear;
with your proboscis shining through the night,
you'll lead my sleigh's traditional team of deer."
Thus Rudolph's gleaming nose brought Christmas joy
and gifts to every girl and every boy.

Wendy Fletcher
ENGLAND

Wendy grew up in the Cambridgeshire fens, living in a pair of Great Eastern Railway carriages, built in 1887 and bought by her grandparents in 1935. She still lives in the carriages today, and last year she published a memoir of her childhood *The Railway Carriage Child*. She is also editor of the *Whittlesey Way*, the local U3A magazine, and set up and runs the local writing group, The Whittlesey Wordsmiths. Wendy is currently writing her first novel, a romance/mystery, and compiling a history of Kings Dyke, a thriving community of seventy houses, school, chapel, shop, club, etc., which housed the Itter brickyard workers from the 1890s until the early 1980s when they were demolished. This will include stories from the many families who lived there.

E: wendyfletcherwriting@gmail.com
W: www.wendywordsmith.com
Blog: www.whittleseywordsmiths.com

BOXING DAY IN THE FENS

Boxing Day dawns,
the day of sport,
Across the fields
the air is clear

Jackets buttoned,
Scarves tucked in tight,
hands behind backs
men stoop down low

Then, at the shot
long blades strike out,
Scoring the ice
Fen Runners glide

A glint of steel
in morning sun,
Following banks
lined by willows,

Heads bowed to chest
against the wind,
the skaters head
across the fen

Right to Ramsey
and to Ely,
Left to Crowland
and Thorney too,

they trace the old
route of the Nene,
where the water
flowed to the mere

along frozen
drains and full dykes,
skimming the frost
of silent miles

their steaming breath
marks out the way

of the fastest men
on the fen today

AUTHOR'S NOTE: 'Fen Runners' is the old name for the blades which men attached to their boots, in order to skate across the fens, not only for Boxing day sport but when winter conditions made many areas inaccessible by other means.

MEMORIES FROM AN 1887 GER RAILWAY CARRIAGE.

Christmas 1960
Where was I then?
A carriage child,
A girl of the fen.

On Christmas Eve
We trim the tree,
My parents,
Granny and me.

The embers glow
The baubles shine,
In this carriage
Home of mine.

Tonight I wait,
Silent as the snow,
White beyond windows,
Eight in a row.

Grass grows
Beneath the floor,
Steam is stilled
Buffers clang no more.

But on each step
And in every door,
I feel the presence
Here before.

Carrying troops to war
and sometimes back,
The carriage rolled
On a forgotten track,

goodbyes and promises
To meet again,
I feel the passion
And the pain.

But I wonder now
Does anyone care
about the carriage
that carried them there?

Lisa Molina
USA

Lisa holds a BFA from The University of Texas at Austin, and has taught high school English and Theatre. She was named Teacher of the Year by the Lake Travis ISD Education Foundation in 1992. She also served as Associate Publisher of *Austin Family* magazine. Lisa has published in *Indolent Books - Poems in the Afterglow, Trouvaille Review, Eris & Eros Review, Sad Girls Literary Blog*, and will have poems featured soon in *Tiny Seed Literary Journal*, and *Academy of the Heart and Mind.* Her life changed forever when her son battled leukaemia three times over seven years, and still has numerous health issues as a result of the treatments. Since 2000, Molina has worked with students with special needs, both at the pre-K and high school levels. When not reading and writing, she can be found singing, playing piano, or hiking. She finds peace being near any body of water, especially the beach. She believes art and nature are essential to the life of the soul. She lives in Austin, Texas with her family and cat.
E: lisabmolina@gmail.com

CHRISTMAS OF LIGHTS

T'was the night before Christmas...

Our 3 year old cancer-fighter in Superman pyjamas,
Hanging on to life by a thread,
Will it hold?

Untethered from IV pumps on the paediatric cancer floor,
Allowed to go home one night only:
Christmas Eve.

"His last?"
We ask ourselves silently.

Snakelike tube still protruding from his chest
So I may connect the IV bag hanging over his bed,

Will he dream of sugarplums dancing in his now bald head?

Wishing Santa will bring more trains for his set,
and perhaps superheroes - Batman, Superman -?
(Much like the super-chemo-heroes
valiantly battling leukaemia cell villains inside of him).

While Saint Nick is packing his sleigh full of toys,
We pack up our car full of medical supplies.

A small Christmas tree awaits in the house,
and stockings we hung on the fireplace with care,
With hopes that good blood counts soon would be there.

When turning the corner to our home,
What do I see?

"A hallucination?"
I ask myself,
"From sleep deprivation?"

We approach slowly.
My lips lifting to a smile.
While warm, salty tears blur the vision of my eyes;

My husband laughing, giggling to our son,

"Look, Andrew, Look!"

I turn to look as his puffy eyes open.
Disoriented by the drugs,
His voice whispers,
"Home."

We stop,
To gawk.
And gaze,
Amazed.

White
      Bright
            Light

Illuminates the long-barren home.

Glimmering,
Glowing.
Despair lifting,
Going -

We get out of the car and stand on the grass.
Husband holding our son tightly to his chest,
Our faces reflect the bright gleaming light.

Clear air cools.
Bright moon shines.
Stars twinkle overhead.

Our first cancer-Christmas
Breaks through the gloom.
By the simple act of friends.
House shining under the moon.

Now hope firmly held and bathed in
Pure white.
I look to the stars dangling, illuminating the night.
And once again,
Believe.

Gabriela Nikoloska
MACEDONIA

Gabriela is a 21 year-old emerging poet from Prilep in Macedonia. She has completed her secondary education and is engaged in studying and writing poetry and prose.
E: gabi99nikoloska@gmail.com

CHRISTMAS

On an Orthodox holiday
which is called Christmas
a boy was born
in the name of Jesus.
Jesus who in himself
holds a goodness
which all of us today
does not caress.
It was snowing that day
which we rejoice in
on that day there is a full table
on which we are all sitting together
smiling and happy
and full of peace and tranquillity
because it is our Orthodox holiday
Christmas which we celebrate in the presence of Jesus
a holiday in which we all find ourselves and unite.

Anita Haas
SPAIN / CANADA

Anita is a differently-abled, award-winning Canadian writer and teacher based in Madrid, Spain. She has published books on film, two novelettes, a short story collection, and articles, poems and fiction in both English and Spanish. Some publications her poetry has appeared in include *Quantum Leap, River Poets Journal, Poetry Quarterly, Vox Poetica, Verse Virtual, Wink, Songs of Eretz, Parody Magazine, Silver Birch, Madness Muse* and *Founder's Favourites*. She spends her free time watching films, and enjoying tapas and flamenco with her writer husband and two cats.

E: aephaas@hotmail.com

THE PRESENT

On a cold white Christmas long ago
A friend gave me a present.
Ooh and Ahh I told him then,
"How kind, how sweet, how pleasant."

At once I started on my scheme
To pass the present on.
I had no use for this old junk
And it didn't take me long.

So soon I found my lucky chance
and gave it to a friend.
I thought I'd seen the last of it,
And that had been the end.

But little did I know it then
My friend would follow suit
And soon the gift was sent again
Along its merry route.

Round and round the present went
Passed along the chain,
Of family, friends, acquaintances
And back to me again!

First published in *Parody Magazine*, 2014.

David Milley
USA

David has written and published verse since the 1970s, while building a career as a technical writer and web applications developer. His work has appeared in *Painted Bride Quarterly, Christopher Street*, and *Bay Windows*. Retired now, David lives in southern New Jersey with his husband of four decades, Warren Davy, who's made his living as a farmer, woodcutter, nurseryman, beekeeper, and cook. These days, Warren tends his garden and keeps honeybees, while David walks and writes.
E: daveweb@davidmilley.com
W: www.davidmilley.com

WARMING WINTER
(Christmas Day, 2016)

I look out the window at the yard. The sun silhouettes
bare wood on rain trees, lights up ivy climbing pine.
No snow again this year; the squirrels get fat on suet
meant for the birds, who, this year, find finer fare to dine.

Across the table, Warren looks up from his breakfast,
catches my eyes above my scrolling screen. I grin;
he shakes his head and returns to his meal. Long past
needing to explain, he finishes, gets up, and goes back in.

Past my screen roll greetings that my family and friends
make to the world, announcing where we are today,
and with whom, and what we do. As the long year ends,
we speak to mark this moment in many myriad ways.

Warren fetches new suet for the feeder. As he walks by,
his fingers brush my shoulder. The sun will soon rise high.

Xe M. Sánchez
SPAIN

Xe was born in 1970 in Grau (Asturies, Spain). He received his Ph.D in History from the University of Oviedo in 2016, he is anthropologist, and he also studied Tourism and three masters. He has published in Asturian language *Escorzobeyos* (2002), *Les fueyes tresmanaes d'Enol Xivares* (2003), *Toponimia de la parroquia de Sobrefoz. Ponga* (2006), *Llué, esi mundu paralelu* (2007), *Les Erbíes del Diañu* (E-book: 2013, Paperback: 2015), *Cróniques de la Gandaya* (E-book, 2013), *El Cuadernu Prietu* (2015), and several publications in journals and reviews in Asturies, USA, Portugal, France, Sweden, Scotland, Australia, South Africa, India, Italy, England, Canada, Reunion Island, China, Belgium, Ireland and Netherlands.
E: sanchez.xe.m@gmail.com

COVETING JANUARY

Christmas celebrations
are approaching again
step by step.
It is a suitable time
to remember
that we have been children
a long time ago
and also, to remember
our absences.
It is time to remember
that we are still not only
- at best -
a memory
or a photograph.
This poisoned year,
the best Christmas gift
will be, for sure, the New Year.
We will only be living ghosts
if we forget
our hopes.

Masudul Hoq
BANGLADESH

Masudul has a PhD in Aesthetics under Professor Hayat Mamud at Jahangirnagar University, Dhaka. He is a contemporary Bengali poet, short story writer, translator and researcher. His previous published work includes short stories; *Tamakbari* (1999), The poems *Dhonimoy Palok* (2000), *Dhadhashil Chaya,* of which the translated version is *Shadow of Illusion* (2005), and *Jonmandher Swapna,* of which the translated version is *Blind Man's Dream* (2010, translated by Kelly J. Copeland). Masudul has also translated from English to Bengali T.S. Eliot's poem *Four Quartets* (2012) and Allen Ginsburg's poem *Howl* (2018). In the late 1990s, he worked for three years under a research fellowship at The Bangla Academy, which has published his two research books. His poems have been published in the Chinese, Romanian ,Mandarin, Azarbaijanese, Turkish, Nepali and Spanish languages. At present he is a Professor of Philosophy at a government college.
E: masudul.hoq@gmail.com

HAPPINESS

Our village is further east across the Himalayas
Wandering in the Zhou and Devdaru forests
The fog comes to the village by touching the ice
We find the shadow of good fortune in it
When winter comes, we look north
Kanchenjunga surrounded by clouds is hanging in the sky
This time in December
In the garland of light awakened in the fog
I will decorate the forest with zhao and fir trees
If any happy bird before the Christmas
comes flying towards our village
we will decorate the forest with zhao and fir trees

DECEMBER TWENTY-FIVE

Shepherd and I are two brothers in human birth
He and I were born in December
He is before; I am after
While protecting the wood industry from damage
He became the Jesus of the cross long before me!

After much later I cry loudly for the pain
Of losing my brother while reading holy scripts.
I think this time in our northern hemisphere
When the twenty-fifth of December will come by lighting the festival
brightness
I will make the small day bigger!

Mark O. Decker
USA

Writing poetry has been a part of Mark's life for over 50 years. When he retired in 2016, he decided to organize his poetry and share it with family and friends. The response was incredibly positive and emboldened him to try to reach out to a broader audience with hopes that his words will touch, encourage, inspire others. He also wants his grandchildren, which now number nine, to know him in a very spiritual way that is difficult to convey otherwise.

E: mdeckersr@gmail.com
Instagram: @Okeypoet

CHRISTMAS

Christmas means home fires burning,
in our hearts,
flames leaping
at the thought of little children;
Being together as grown-ups,
laughing and loving, without fear,
like our moms and dads did,
yesterday, when our lives
were wrapped around
their hearts and thoughts;
They were our inspiration
as we are, now, to the little ones,
who wrap themselves,
so dearly, around us;
So near to Christmas time are we, and
we are nearer to each other
In this holy Christmas time;
Nearer to our Maker,
and each other.

CHRISTMAS AT HOME

Santa, we've proclaimed,
will come on Monday, and
we have discussed the story
of Joseph, Mary and baby Jesus
while we gazed, in awe,
at our warm and beautiful tree,
that signifies what is to be,
joy, prayer and serenity;
The nutcracker plays forward,
both young and grown child
dance toward;
The familiar songs draw, in us,
a sense of grace;
Life will show Santa to our door,
love will ask him to ignore
Our imperfections,
the human foibles
that here are stored.

Bhuwan Thapaliya
NEPAL

Nepalese poet, is the author of four poetry collections *Safa Tempo: Poems New and Selected, Our Nepal, Our Pride, Rhythm of the Heart* and *Verses from the Himalayas*, and is currently working on his latest collection *The Marching Millions*. He is a prolific poet and is writing his own Everest, and spreading the message of global peace, universal solidarity and love. Bhuwan has read his poetry and attended seminars in venues around the world, including South Korea, the United States, Thailand, Cambodia, and Nepal, and his work has been widely published in leading literary journals, newspapers and periodicals such as *Kritya, The Foundling Review, ApekshaNews, Strong Verse, Counercurrents.org, myrepublica, The Kashmir Pulse, Taj Mahal Review, Nuveine Magazine, Poetry Life and Times, Ponder Savant, VOICES(Education Project), The Vallance Review, Longfellow Literary Project, Poets Against the War* and others. His poetries have also been published in the CD's and Books such as T*he New Pleiades Anthology of Poetry, Tonight: An Anthology of World Love Poetry* and *The Strand Book of International Poets 2010* and many more.
E: nepalipoet@yahoo.com

WHEN WILL MY CHRISTMAS TREE ARRIVE?

Forlorn and fragile as a shirt
that dangles on the wooden hanger
dropped to the toe of a termite eaten
rack, without a face nor any grace.
And hopeless as a necktie around
the collar of the polyester skeleton,
concentric rings of an agonizing grief.
I am passing my days and playing
hide and seek with the death.
The coronavirus has changed
my mind in many ways.
My hearts heritage
can't easily be reassembled.
Nevertheless, as this grim year
comes to its close.
I want to hug. I want to smile.
I want to chatter on and on.
I want to have a feast.
I want to be with them all again.
I am desperately waiting
for the Christmas this year.
When will my
Christmas tree arrive?
I want it quickly.
The dexterous stitches
of my emotional hook
may break soon.

Luisa Kay Reyes
USA

Luisa has had pieces featured in *The Raven Chronicles, The Windmill, The Foliate Oak, The Eastern Iowa Review*, and other literary magazines. Her essay, *Thank You*, is the winner of the April 2017 memoir contest of The Dead Mule School Of Southern Literature, and her Christmas poem was a first place winner in the 16th Annual Stark County District Library Poetry Contest. Additionally, her essay *My Border Crossing* received a Pushcart Prize nomination from the Port Yonder Press, and two of her essays have been nominated for the Best of the Net anthology, with one of her essays recently being featured on *The Dirty Spoon* radio hour.
E: LuisaKayReyes@gmail.com

THE EVE OF GOODNESS AND MIGHT

Whether commissioned by a committee
To celebrate a Christmas in the City
The German carol "O Christmas Tree"
Can be sung from Berlin to the South China Sea.

While the hills may seem out of reach
When celebrating Christmas at the beach
The spiritual "Go, Tell It On The Mountains"
Is hummed while throwing pennies in the fountains.

And a Country Christmas is never complete
Without some pies that are tasty and sweet
For the upbeat Welsh tune "Deck the Hall"
Is pleasant for feasting right before nightfall.

With scarves and some muffs in some horse-drawn sleighs
A Victorian Christmas cures one's malaise
As the Sussex air "On Christmas Night"
Lingers softly amidst the candlelight.

Caring compassion for the infirm and destitute
During a Dickens Christmas is far from moot
Making generosity alive and well
Throughout the French tune "The First Noel".

The eve, The Light and The Way were unfurled
Is hailed by Handel in "Joy to the World"
And reflecting upon the Austrian strains of "Silent Night"
The universe is filled with Christ's goodness and might.

Kathleen Boyle
VIETNAM / ENGLAND.

Now based in Vietnam, Kathleen Boyle (nee Dodd), was born in Liverpool, England, where she spent her childhood years before leaving to train as a teacher in Hull. Kathleen then worked as a teacher in Hull, Leeds, London and Carlisle, and at international schools in Colombia, Bahrain, Cairo, Armenia and Vietnam. She has written stories and poems throughout her life, and published a collection of poems about growing up in 1950s Liverpool entitled, *Sugar Butties and Mersey Memoirs*, as well as a collection of poems for children about a teddy bear called *Harry Pennington*. During her time in Bahrain she wrote *The Pearl House*, a short story which spans the cultural divides of Liverpool and Bahrain. While teaching in Cairo, Kathleen published her novella, *Catherine of Liverpool,* and while teaching in Vietnam, has completed her recent book *The Storyteller of Cotehill Wood*.

E: kathdodd@aol.com

THE CHRISTMAS TREES OF WARWICK ROAD
(Written after floods devastated Carlisle, UK)

For years now,
On the slow and dismal mid-winter
Trawl to work and back,
Shuffling through the darkness in the car,
The Christmas trees of Warwick Road
Have sparkled through the gloom,
Have entertained bored children,
As we inched our way through
Endless roadworks.
We would study them,
And choose the one we liked the best.
Like clock-work they appeared,
Lovely in the windows,
Lights and baubles blazing,
A credit to their owners,
We always loved,
The Christmas trees of Warwick Road
Throughout the year,
As I have passed those houses,
Broken and deserted,
I have often thought about the Christmas trees,
And their owners,
I know they will return,
And as we pass along the road again,
We'll smile a special welcome,
To the Christmas trees of Warwick Road.

'TWAS THE FRIGHT BEFORE CHRISTMAS

'Twas Christmas Eve and all was well
I put my child to bed,
and on the hearth mince pie and milk
for Santa to be fed.

The moon shone bright, I smiled that night,
for all my work was done.
'Twas time to put my feet up now
and wait for Christmas fun.

I settled down to watch T.V.
Now life could not be better,
'twas while I sought remote controls
I came across a letter.

'Twas written by my little one
in gold and as I read,
the peace I felt deserted me,
to my distress it said;

'Dear Santa Clause, Hello to you
I hope you're feeling well.
There's only one thing I would like
and that's a silver bell.

I've kept this wish a secret.
Only you and I will know
I hope you'll make my dream come true
because I trust you so.'

'Twas almost midnight Christmas Eve
and panic filled the night.
Wherever would I find a bell?
My Christmas joy took flight.

I searched the house to no avail,
'twas absolutely fruitless.
So went to bed, it must be said
I felt completely useless.

'Twas Christmas morn, my little one
came to my room to tell

that Santa Clause had brought for her
a lovely silver bell!

Now every Christmas Eve I write
a note to Santa Clause,
and thank him for the silver bell.
'Twas worthy of applause.

CUMBRIAN CHRISTMAS

Getting through another winter,
Bone cold, damp lunged,
They trim the tree and stick,
Bright snowmen,
To frosted glass,

While on a rain soaked,
Cumbrian landscape,
Sheep bleat in the dark.
Cosy indoors,
Christmas is underway.

Jane Blanchard
USA

Jane lives and writes in Georgia. Her poetry has appeared in venues around the world - both in print and online - with recent work in *The French Literary Review, The Lyric, The Seventh Quarry*, and *THINK*. Her latest collection is *In or Out of Season* (2020).
E: JEGBlanchard@aol.com

CHRISTMAS

As long foretold
By prophets old,
An infant child,
Both meek and mild,
Was born this day
Upon the hay
In stable dim
At Bethlehem.

As angel throngs
Did carol songs,
The shepherds feared,
A star appeared,
And wise men stared,
Then far they dared
To ride in joy
To see a boy.

Thus, God above
In wondrous love
Did send His son
To everyone
Of human race
Who seeks His grace
So none will miss
Eternal bliss.

First published in *The Shepherd's Voice*, and republished in Tides & Currents (2017).

Patrick O'Shea
NETHERLANDS / UK

Patrick is both British and Dutch and lives in Rijswijk, Holland. He is retired and a widower, who find writing to be a most satisfying part of his life, and is constantly trying to improve his quality in writing, while considering the social world we are all living in. He has been fortunate to have some pieces published in *The Greensilk Journal* (USA), as well as *Vaughan Street Doubles* (Saskatchewan, Canada). He is concerned about the split in societies around the world, and the lack of openness in discussions, resulting in failure in understanding. He does, however, find great hope in the humanity in people he has seen around the world, not unsurprisingly among those with the least. His wish is that his writing may help others to question their life and either accept who they are, or seek change.
E: patrick@copas.demon.nl

THE SEASON

The rich smell of fresh cut pine trees garners the memories from out of the air,
As all the many packages are wrapped by so many hands, all with love and care,
Bright lights shine on dark streets and in towns, growing in presence all around,
While the open laughter and the happy voices become a more frequent sound.

With the food on the plates, come some loudly whispered adulation of the cook,
So many past seasons meals shared in memory during eating, with just a quiet look,
The presently beloved food being absorbed hungrily with openly shared joy, in the way,
That this time wraps the gathering warmly, showing bright reflections of a happy day.

The holly and the ivy are quietly waiting together for admirers, against trees and walls,
As the families and friends get ready to walk out in the cold with mufflers and shawls,
The well-known seasonal carols gather volume from all the voices that are now all singing,
And these old songs are so well accompanied by all the bells that are joining in ringing.

Tis the season we know of old, and provides the reason that we can try to understand,
That peace and tranquillity are not to be ignored or eschewed, but not always at hand,
For what we may find truly in our own heart's depth is what we all may come to know,
That life in this lovely season can quite openly be shared, and easily leave all with a glow.

A CHRISTMAS SEASON

Across the streets of darkness, a warmth insinuates itself quietly into the life of the passer-by, in the
Season of lights we now begin to visit and know again,
Lights have been strung on a tall tree without any leaves, and they transmute that empty tree into a
Nightly vision of a tall Christmas tree, a nightly friend,
The darkness of the time of year is held at bay, any cold is not so very cold after all as one begins to
Explore the streets and discover more beauty there,
Peering into houses as one walks the streets, is to discover the joy that is being shared, the happiness
That is part of the time of year, the simple way to care.

Poinsettias begin to grace the inside of houses with their lovely red colour, balanced again their fine dark
Green leaves, and faces smile when they are seen,
Children of all ages begin to wonder what they will find if they are most lucky, under the Christmas tree,
And their faces reflect the hope and their dream,
Music drifts through so many houses carrying the sounds that so many will know from their own early
Days of life, and the sounds carry the memory of olden times,
The songs that are being sung, and the voices that sing them again, carry thoughts through the season,
And there is so much emotion wrapped up in those rhymes.

There is a certain quietness descending upon houses, streets, and cities as the day known as Christmas Day comes closer in time, but there is laughter mixed in and nothing is rote,
For the season is always renewed, is always refreshed, how can it ever be seen as old, for just as there
Is another day, the world can hear the sound of love, that special note,
There is nothing more wonderful than to see people smiling, full of a joy that may be missed at another
Time of the year, but now lights the faces in these days,
It is a time of the year, a chance to reflect, a time to dance and sing, a chance to give thanks for another
Year, it is a time to come to know a Christmas season and its ways.

STEP TOE MISTLETOE

Step toe, mistletoe, just dancing in the breeze,
Laughing children all down upon their knees,
Radiant balls of colour that easily light upon the eye,
Lights so bright within the night just held up by sky,
Branches of fir here and there are shown with care
A gathering of merriment, a partridge and a pear.

Step toe, mistletoe, give the child a kiss and a squeeze,
Warmth in the smiles, happy caring no bad disease,
Poinsettia just redly cheeky, and sits quite neatly
In a house, in a winter's tale, joining green so sweetly,
Cards left hanging, with the kind words still dangling,
The messages sent and received, joy in the bringing.

Step toe, mistletoe, now floating in the world of trees,
The memories flow through the self with casual ease,
Ornaments shown with the history of the many years,
The worries hung up and put away quietly, in joy no fears,
A pound and a penny, always a warm drink here for any,
A dance around the mistletoe, a kiss, new hope for many.

Chrys Salt MBE
ENGLAND / SCOTLAND

Based between London and Edinburgh, Chrys is a seasoned performer and a widely published and anthologized poet. She has performed in festivals across the UK, in Europe, America, Canada, Finland and India, and written in almost every genre except the novel. Numerous awards include a National Media Award, an Arts and Business Award, Several Writing Bursaries and a Fringe First from The Edinburgh Festival. She has published seven books for actors, and nine poetry collections. She is Artistic Director of BIG LIT: The Stewartry Book Festival, a five day literary festival in SW Scotland now in its ninth year. Chrys was awarded an MBE in the Queen's Birthday Honours List for Services to The Arts.

E: chrys@chryssalt.com
W: www.chryssalt.com
W: www.biglit.org

DAFFODILS AT CHRISTMAS

Gay as a blackbird's beak
your daffodils unbud
and burst into frilled trumpets
this Christmas morning,
bringing a torch of freshness
to the season's ritual,
reminding the heart's cold bulb
of its green, forgotten centre.
Better to have left the corner bare
than focus this bright beam
on the chill comfort I have grown to.
Better not to dare
this incandescent flame
for fear its clear and unexpected shining
blinds me into love,
and, sweeter then sap, your gentleness
enters my bones
calling my roots to draw up joy again

FLORENCE 1903 -2006

I saw her last on Christmas day -
kissed her egg shell skull
pearly under a froth of new perm
like a butterfly
landing .
Her woody fingers sprouted
nails as bright as berries for the season
her feet a pair of too-big slippers
furry and brand new.
She was going to a nephew
in Edinburgh she said for turkey.
She thought the tree with the lights on
was lovely
and the flowers sent
by a Jamaican lady
were lovely
and the little brooch I gave her
- that was lovely too.

Back from my holiday
she wasn't there
someone I didn't know was in her chair
nodding and smiling.
Heart grief came hot, quick,
suddenly spilling over
and – typical - no hanky!

I saw her last on Christmas day.

She thought everything was lovely.

She was wearing her best
'going-to-church-in' blue.

WALTZ TIME AT CHRISTMAS

they're doing the Alzheimer Waltz
the one two three Alzheimer Waltz
the tune is an oldie
beyond all recall
but they pivot and twirl
on a sixpence of dreams
his suit double breasted
her stockings with seams
all sense disconnected
unplugged from the wall
they're doing the Alzheimer Waltz

waltz of forgetfulness
danced in a wilderness
caught between
somewhere and been there before
they know all the steps
but can't think what they're for
in the
one two three
Alzheimer Waltz

they're doing the Alzheimer Waltz
the one two three Alzheimer Waltz
on snub slippered feet

that forget they remember
the dance tunes of spring-time
in dying December
they shimmy and swirl
light fantastic unerring
a dashing young soldier
a slip of a girl
in the
one two three
Alzheimer Waltz

waltz of forgetfulness
danced in a wilderness
caught between
somewhere and been there before
they know all the steps
but can't think what they're for
in the one two three Alzheimer Waltz
they're doing The Alzheimer Waltz.
the one two three Alzheimer Waltz
and the lights on the tree
are as bright as the light
in the eyes of the dancers
who take to the floor
in the one two three
one two three
one two three
one two three
one two three Alzheimer Waltz

Pat Smekal
CANADA

Pat lives by the sea on Vancouver Island, B.C. She fills her life with family, friends, travel, laughter and of course words. Since 2003, Pat's poetry has won a number of prizes and has appeared in more than seventy publications in Canada and abroad. In 2009 her chapbook *Praise without Mortar* was launched. In 2012 *Small Corners* (2012), and in 2013 *Maybe We Could Dance*, in collaboration with David Fraser, were published. Another collaboration with fellow poet Ian Cognito resulted in the book *flora fauna & h. sapiens* (2019), and *Much Ado about Nothing* (2020). A long-standing member of The WordStorm Society of the Arts and the B.C Federation of Writers, Pat has frequently read her poetry at spoken-word events on Vancouver Island and beyond.
E: jazzsmekal@shaw.ca

CHRISTMAS KITCHEN MEMORIES

We watch and wait, while Mister Ames,
early on the twenty-fifth,
delivers the turkey.
Unplucked and decidedly dead, it lies
limp on the chopping-board, surrounded
by an expanse of white Formica.

Wearing her red and green apron,
Mother rolls up her sleeves,
starts with boiling water.
After the bird's plunge, she begins
the plucking... always
one, two, three pulls
for a handful, until her bucket
is full of wet feathers.

The window takes her eyes
from time to time, as she listens
for the gate's squeaky hinges
and Nannie's stolid step
on the back stairs. Nannie,
who will bring sage, thyme,
sweet onion, celery leaves
and two-day old bread
for the stuffing.

We watch Mother shape a taper
from inside pages of the Province.
She sets it alight, holds the bird
over the stainless-steel sink
by one drumstick, singes
its left-over pin-feathers. The
familiar, pleasant scent of it
hangs around, tantalizing.

At last, from the porch,
Nannie calls out,"Merry Christmas!"
and nudges her stocky frame inside.
We already know the wicker basket
she holds will be chock full of goodies.

Wansoo Kim
SOUTH KOREA

Wansoo achieved Ph.D. in English Literature from the graduate school of Hanguk University of Foreign Studies. He was a lecturer at Hanguk University of Foreign Studies, and an adjunct professor at Incheon Junior College for about 20 years. He has published five poetry books, one novel, and one book of essays. One poetry book, *Duel among a middle-aged fox, a wild dog and a deer* was a bestseller in 2012, one page from the book of *Letters for Teenagers* was put in textbooks of middle school (2011) and high school (2014) in South Korea, and four books (*Easy-to-read English Bible stories, Old Testament* (2017), *New Testament* (2018) and *Teenagers, I Support your Dream*) were bestsellers. He was granted a Rookie award for poetry at the magazine of *Monthly Literature Space* in South Korea, and the World Peace Literature Prize for Poetry Research and Recitation, presented in New York City at the 5th World Congress of Poets(2004). He published poetry books, *Prescription of Civilization* and *Flowers of Thankfulness in America*.(2019), received Geum-Chan Hwang Poetry Literature Prize in Korea (2019) and International Indian Award (literature) from WEWU (World English Writer's Union)(2019).
E: ws91912@hanmail.net

CHRISTMAS EVE

Here and there in front of the shopping area,
False Santas
Shake their handbell to open wallets,

Into the red mouth of a motel
That the electric sign with 'Merry Christmas' glitters,
Staggering young boys and girls are sucked,

At the corner of a subway station a Salvationist shakes a handbell,
The red frozen hands of a crouching homeless person
Are trembling due to the glares of the crowd,

In public houses, drunken people
Beat on the table with their chopsticks to carols
Chewing Jesus as a side dish,

In the nightclubs on the back streets,
Men and women intoxicated by light and music
Are burning their whole body and soul as a living sacrifice to Bacchus,

But in the sky, the tears of Jesus, snowing in large flakes
Pat all the people regardless of the homeless, the drunken, age or sex
Like mothers' hands.

Colette Tennant
USA

Colette is an English professor living in Salem, Oregon. She has two books of poetry *Commotion of Wings* and *Eden and After.* Her poems have been published in various journals including *Prairie Schooner, Rattle*, and P*oetry Ireland Review*. Her most recent book is *Religion in The Handmaid's Tale: A Brief Guide*, published in 2019 to coincide with Atwood's publication of *The Testaments*.
E: CTennant@corban.edu
FB: @colette.tennant

CHRISTMAS PAST

Why do I always go back
to the ribbon candy?
Hard and shaped like
green and red sleigh runners.

And we had a pink Christmas tree,
Its colour doing happy handstands,
content cartwheels all through the house.

A Christmas tree pink as a newborn
pink as a baby's pink ears
filled with carols
and all sorts of full-breasted love.

Annmarie H. Pearson
USA

Born in 1949 in Fitchburg, Massachusetts, Annmarie is a poet, novelist, fibre artist, a Reiki Master/Teacher, and a Tai Chi and Qigong enthusiast. She is a University of New Mexico alumni, and once received a New Mexico Governor's Volunteer Award. She is a mother, grandmother, and a spouse to a wonderful family. She resides in New Mexico for over fifty years with her husband. She is an active member in her poetry community at the New Mexico State Poetry Society (Rio Grande Poets Chapter), and in the New Mexico Poetry Alliance. She has been published in many diverse publications including: the *Playboy* magazine, the *Valencia County News-Bulletin*, the *University of New Mexico Valley Visions*, *World Healing/World Peace* publication, and in many anthologies.
E: altbalance@q.com

OLD MAN WINTER

Breath becomes mist as one speaks
Ice forms on a slow-moving creek
Leaves have fallen to the ground
As winter wind twirls them around

Women knit warm woolly shawls
While men bundle-up in snug-tight-thermals
Life eagerly transforms to a seasonal bliss
And the cold arctic changes in Aurora Borealis

Snow graces the frozen ground
With white enchantment abound
Shovels emerge to stubborn minds
Because winter is not always loved in kind

However, winter helps nature sleep
As her children harvest crops to reap
The cycle animates in all beasts
Bears hibernate and men make feasts

We celebrate in winter jamboree
Halloween, Thanksgiving, and Christmas glee
For it is our time to share in love and gratitude
As we consider Old Man Winter a beatitude

A CHILD'S CONCEPT OF CHRISTMAS

A grown-up once told me
that Christmas was all in the spirit.
What does that mean? Is Christmas a ghost?

I thought Christmas meant joy -
it is joyous to give gifts to mummy and daddy
as my gleeful eyes fill with elation
when hearing my parents give oozes and aahs
after they open their presents of love.

I thought Christmas meant excitement -
it is exciting to receive toys of yearning
my heart fills with enchantment and happiness
as I rip open colourful wrappings
and look for another gift under the decorated tree.

I thought Christmas meant fulfilment -
it is the deliciously scrumptious meals
served by grandma, mummy, and auntie
tasting the mouth-watering entrées
and anticipating deserts of cakes, cookies, and pies.

I thought Christmas meant merriment -
with laughter and glee in listening to all the stories
by grandpa, daddy, and uncle
as they relate their experiences
each story wilder, funnier, and some unreal
as the grown-ups try to top their next tale.

I thought Christmas meant amusement -
playing games with siblings and parents
and hearing screams of fun, laughter, and cheer
while children hustle and bustle in playful activities
as I watch my parents savour the precious moments.

I think I understand what that grown-up was trying to say:
"Christmas is in the spirit of life - in giving, in sharing, and loving."
It is meant for all eternity, not only for just one day.
So, I say Merry Christmas to all, forever and ever, and every day.

MY FIRST CHRISTMAS AS A MRS.

Many, many years ago, I remember my first Christmas as a Mrs.,
it was a glorious sailor's glow when I assisted St. Nicholas.
It was in the year nineteen sixty-nine just short of three days
of our first anniversary. I married at the innocent age of nineteen.
I was twenty by the time our first Christmas came around.

My husband's ship docked at Mare Island just outside the San
Francisco Bay. The USS Paricutin, an ammunition ship, returned
from its many tours from our nation's war with Viet Nam.
So many sailors were stationed at the docked port in
California, without leave for the holiday season.

My husband asked if I would cook a Christmas feast for about eight
of his ship mates, who were unable to return to their homes for
the holidays. I remember a huge turkey filled with stuffing, and
all the holiday trimmings, including our first Christmas tree.

The table was set with mixed matched dishes and odds-and-ends
silverware. Our furniture came from friends, and many second-hand
stores. The merry meal lasted for over an hour as no one wanted to
leave the festive table. All the sailors pitched in to help in the kitchen,
there was no food left-over to refrigerate.

When we all returned to the crowded living room, all seats were
filled by a sailor, and some sat on the floor. One sailor, I remember
his name as Frank, picked up a twelve-string guitar, and he played
it most beautifully. Before he ended his solo performance,
he encored with Christmas holiday melodies.

To my surprise, a sailor began to sing as the rest of us joined
in with more Christmas carols. When the evening came to an end,
they all thanked me for being their Mrs. Claus. Today, I
wonder if any of those sailors have ever pondered on that
Christmas day of nineteen sixty-nine, a time when I was
only twenty, with dreamy anticipation of our first anniversary.

It was a time where I had innocently hoped to please my
husband, and to please his homesick sailor mates, as I truly
enjoyed pretending to be Mrs. Santa Claus.

Tessa Thomson
ENGLAND

Tessa always felt that she had latent writing potential. But not until her 74th birthday did she finally decide to do something about it. She joined a small writing group and set about her first project with enthusiasm. The project set for that month at the group was "What did you do yesterday?" which started her journey as a poet. Tessa continues to write in verse from her home in Wimblington, north Cambridgeshire, which she shares with working cocker spaniels Lewis and Swallow, and husband Wally.
E: tessathomson1@gmail.com
W: www.tessathomsonpoetry.com

A MODERN CHRISTMAS TALE

Christmas is a time of joy,
But not for me and my little boy.
As we pace the streets with dog in tow,
Hoping for kindness and someone to show
They care just for once, about how we live,
Consciences sated by pennies they give.

The *Big Issue* copies freeze in our hands.
The pittance we make, the hours we stand.
We sleep in a doorway but never there twice,
Moving along, a bench might suffice.
Food is a luxury we can't always afford.
We have no money for bed and for board.

We look out for people who might take my boy,
Not caring that he is my one only joy,
That he is my life and my reason to live,
The one thing I'll fight for, the last thing I'll give
For someone to raise him as they do see fit.
It's the promise I made: that we'll never be split.

Last Christmas we lived in a beautiful home.
Ours was a lifestyle others might own.
It came at a price few outside had known.
Friends thought perhaps I was accident prone.
For years I had covered the marks on my skin
Swearing I'd fallen or been on the gin.

Not once did they question the man in my life.
The charming and genial husband and wife.
We posed as the couple so perfect in bliss,
But ours was a marriage in total amiss.
His drinking, his anger, the sorrow next day.
The pitiful crying the tears would betray.

Then came my child, such joy I knew then,
But soon I could tell it was mayhem again.
He started on me where my clothing could hide,
But once he was angry and he hit my child.
That was the moment I promised to leave.

That was the moment the plan was conceived.

With presents wrapped pretty and under the tree
We acted all's well, my boy and me.
While planning on leaving as night-time befell,
Unsure of our future away from this hell.
Christmas would never be quite the same
But we'd spend it together, not pawns in his game.

It's Christmas again and we're weary from travel.
It seems like a lifetime we've trudged on this gravel.
But there up ahead is a bright shining light,
A door that is open, a man sees our plight.
A stable with hay and some blankets for warmth.
Now planning can start as our lives we transform.

A YULETIDE WISH

With days now shortened, light draws in,
Afternoons darkened, winter begins.
Seasons of richness now fading away,
Giving flight to the pleasures of long stretched out days.

Now days are much shorter, nights long and cold,
Chilling the bodies, and bones in the old.
Forcing them indoors to sit by the fire,
Till gazing at embers their eyes do retire.

But winters hold pleasures for those brave enough,
To venture outside with gloves and warm muff,
Cross open fens with wide open skies,
See glorious sunsets; the end of day prize.

God chose this time for the birth of his son,
To a stable, shepherds and kings would come.
To kneel and give praise to our saviour, and Lord,
His bountiful blessings upon us he poured.

This time is called Christmas, a time of delight,
When families, and neighbours, and friends all unite.
With carols and verses and cards sent by post,
But I'm missing you, so I'll make this toast.

MERRY CHRISTMAS TO ALL OF YOU, AND PEACE TO THE WORLD
LET LOVE BE YOUR GUIDE AS THE NEW YEAR UNFURLS.

Alexia Kalogeropoulou
GREECE

Alexia was born in Athens, Greece, where she works and lives. She writes mostly in Greek. She has published two poetry books and a non-fiction and she has contributed in many collections of poetry and short stories. Her poems and stories have been published in various national literature magazines and anthologies. She is the founder of BookSitting, a Greek website about books, arts and ideas.

E: alexia.kalogeropoulou@gmail.com
W: www.BookSitting.gr

CHRISTMAS EVE

As I am laying by the fireplace
near the Christmas tree
starring at the firewood
hugged deathly by the flames
that grow stronger
even with the softest breath of fresh air,
and the sparkles
are lighting up my face
defining accurately my shadows,
I am thinking of you, my love,
the warmth
as you embrace my body
with the overwhelming notes of your music
that can't stop playing
even when you are silent.

Eliza Segiet
POLAND

Eliza graduated with a Master's Degree in Philosophy, and has completed postgraduate studies in Cultural Knowledge, Philosophy, Arts and Literature at Jagiellonian University. Her poems *Questions* and *Sea of Mists* won the *Spillwords Press* title of International Publication of the Year 2017 and 2018, and *Sea of Mists* was chosen as one of the best amidst the hundred best poems of 2018 by *International Poetry Press Publication* Canada. In *The 2019 Poet's Yearbook,* as the author of *Sea of Mists*, she was awarded with the prestigious Elite Writer's Status Award, as one of the best poets of 2019, and her poem *Order* was selected as one of the 100 best poems of 2019. Eliza was nominated for the Pushcart Prize 2019, the iWoman Global Awards 2020, and the Laureate Naji Naaman Literary Prize, 2020. Her works can be found in anthologies and literary magazines worldwide.
E: eliza.anna@op.pl

WANDERER
Translated by Artur Komoter

Can you hear
the murmur of the forest?
In autumn the trees sing,
in the winter
illuminated
they invite to the memories.

Although cut down
– they still look up
they don't bunk down on the moss.
They look out.

The lights blink with dreams.
And they
are still waiting.

Maybe someday
in the murmur of a forest
a lone wanderer will hear the cry?
Maybe someday
they will feel the festive taste?

FESTIVE TABLE
Translated by Artur Komoter

In the memory,
can survive the time.

I remember
the festive table,
the smell of the forest.
I remember
the joy of being together.

Time
– woven with memories.

P.J. Reed
ENGLAND

P.J. Reed is an award-winning, multi-genre author with books ranging from high fantasy, horror, to haiku. She writes the *Richard Radcliffe Paranormal Investigations* series and the *Bad Decisions* series. Reed is also the editor and chief paranormal investigator for the *Exmoor Noir* newsletter. She has also written a series of seasonal haiku collections - *Haiku Yellow, Haiku Gold*, and *Haiku Ice* as well as Flicker one sizzling senryu collection. P.J. lives in Devon with her two daughters, two rescue dogs, and one feral cat called Sammy.
E: pjreedwriting@gmail.com
FB: @p.j.reedauthor
Twitter: @PJReed_author
Poetry blog: www.pjreedwriting.wixsite.com/poetry

CHRISTMAS HAIKU

1.
tinsel-wrapped shops smile
under plastic snowflake falls
Christmas shoppers swarm

2.
wood pigeon couples
perch on holly branches
red berry banquets

3.
little snowflake waits
frozen in a fallen cloud
the world grows silent

Betsy Lawson
USA

Betsy was a retired teacher for twenty years (grades 4 to university level), is now - at age 83 - really enjoying life. Surviving a devastating divorce is what pushed her to write her many poems, which ultimately found their way into her book *Soul Mirrors*. Always a teacher, she hopes these poems also help others to find their own way to happiness and purpose again. Recently she became Vice President for America in the Human Rights Global Peace Councils.
E: betsyl12@yahoo.com

CRITICAL CRAYONS

It was the night
Before Christmas.
Excitement filled the air.
I knew the room
Would soon be filled,
But all I really wanted
Was a new box of crayons,
Sharpened with precise points,
And a brand new colouring book.

I hoped for a book
Of lovely ballet dancers,
Beautiful ballerinas
On toe in flouncy tutus.
I knew it would be there.
Then I would get down
On nine year old knees.

I would
Hour after hour
Wear down the points,
Outline in bold black
Each moving figure,
Create clashing kinetic colours
Until on final survey
My very soul was satisfied.

Bill Cushing
USA

Born into a Navy family, Bill lived in several states as well as the Virgin Islands and Puerto Rico, before moving to California. Because of his experience both in the Navy, and as a marine electrician prior to beginning studies at the University of Central Florida, classmates dubbed him the "blue collar poet." He earned an MFA in writing from Goddard College in Vermont and has recently retired after more than 20 years of teaching in Los Angeles area colleges. Bill's volume of poetry, *A Former Life*, was released by Finishing Line Press in 2019 and was honoured with a Kops-Featherling International Book Award. His chapbook *Music Speaks*, winner of the San Gabriel Valley Poetry Festival chapbook award, has been reformatted with illustrations. Bill's work has been published in print and online by various journals and anthologies, including both volumes of the award-winning *Stories of Music*. Bill facilitates a writing workshop for 9 Bridges writers, and has been nominated for a Pushcart Prize.
E: piscespoet@yahoo.com

THE NATURE OF SNOW

is entirely unnatural:
As it descends
naturally, it seems
to move more sideways
than down
and at the same speed
so that, when
watching it from
an insulated interior,
it becomes difficult to tell
whether it floats down
or the world
rises.
When it falls
during times of sleep
or introspection,
it gives no warning.
Looking up, unaware,
you realize it is just
there - as though the world
has always been
this white
and deep.
It falls, silent, not echoing
on eaves or streets.
It does not crunch
so much
as it squeaks
when shoe soles
press down,
compressing it
into complaints
smothering all sounds
but those resulting
from its own condition.
Drifts create
an anechoic atmosphere:
Even dogs become
more silent
in it. Snow resides
above nature. It grows
in layers -

shifting later
to other shapes:

barricading buildings,
isolating
greenhouses from warmth,
covering
a solitary chair in the
middle of a field.

Snow settles on tree limbs
and leaves
like a soft
white
mould.

SOME NOTES OF A RELIGIOUS NATURE

Jesus was sent
to die for our sins
like some package
from UPS.

He delivered the goods
to humanity
and we delivered him
back to Heaven

battered, beaten,
mutilated.
Some creation
we turned out to be.

Jyotirmaya Thakur
ENGLAND / INDIA

Jyotirmaya is a retired Principal, author of twenty-three books, with many waiting to be published. She is a multi-genre award winner - with more than 200 awards - reviewer, columnist, academician, translator, motivational speaker, and a philanthropist. She holds prestigious positions in many international organisations - literary and humanitarian. Her poems and articles have been published in many international anthologies, and translated into many languages. She exemplifies the ideal that writing is more than just words on paper; it is a means of creating a positive change in the world.
E: jyotirmaya.thakur@gmail.com

CHRISTMAS CHEER

The year is ending,
Night is descending,
Weather is freezing,
The wind is howling,
Rivers still flowing,
Christmas choir singing,
Good memories bouncing,
Lights around flashing,
Slender trees baring,
Angels white clouding,
Buried fences opening,
Borderless roads tolling,
Shadows are trailing,
Sad hearts are sailing,
With church bell pealing,
Mercy is widely feeling,
Kindness in air is filling,
Happiness is awakening,
Plentiful praises preaching,
Travellers truly rocking,
All regions quietly drowning,
In grace of God's blessings.

BE A SANTA TODAY

What the world needs today,
Is a real Santa on its way,
For orphans on streets,
Or ragpickers with dreams.

If you are planning a party
For the rich and savvy friends only,
Who only dine and drink to vomit,
Change your plans and commit,
To feed the beggars on temple stairs,
Sitting in the cold naked and bare.

If you have enough and don't know,
How to join the Christmas show?
How to feel good in festive season?
Just go to slums and give without reason,
While you are lighting the fake fir tree,
Placing a star on top,with white fairies,
There is a child somewhere wanting to be free,
Just walk the extra mile to the drearies.

Save the abandoned humanity roaming,
Old and ailing,homeless without dwelling,
Visit the hospital where patients are waiting,
For a pep talk or company sharing.

Put a smile on a crying child weary,
Lost in the world of injustice teary,
Gifts are enormous not in size but kind,
Be a giver of happiness of the mind.

Be the Santa for whom you waited in childhood,
Let the innocent believe in a Santa of manhood.

Fulfil a dream of starry-eyed innocent,
God blesses the world in guise of benevolent.

Bozena Helena Mazur-Nowak
ENGLAND / POLAND

Originally from Opole in Poland,Bozena moved to England in 2004. She has published seven volumes of poetry: four in Polish and three in English. She also writes prose, and has released a novel and a number of short story collections. Her work can be found in around 100 anthologies and magazines worldwide, and has been translated into 20 languages. She has won many poetry competitions and awards including; the 2015 Maria Konopnicka's award for her merits to the Polish culture, the 2015 Tadeusz Micinski' Expressionist Award, the 2015 St Moniuszko Gold Statuette award for allegiance to Polish culture in her work and its dissemination worldwide, and the 2017 Klemens Janicki Literary Award. Her new volume of poetry book *Carousel of Life* will be published shortly in the USA.
E: bozena.mazur-nowak@hotmail.co.uk
FB: @bozenahelenam

CHRISTMAS

beautiful spruce at neighbour's window
so proud and foster in hundred lanterns
they say that the family will arrive in droves
worry whether enough space for them

and here is so quiet, so quiet
I read the yellowed letters pages
covered with a patina of time

turkey is lazily walking in the garden
and asks for survival

children are looking off frames on the walls
such small and joyful

trembling hands clinging memories to the heart
a wafer is crying on the plate

WAITING FOR THE FIRST STAR

another Christmas is knocking on the door
the tree is no longer as stylish
several unsent Christmas cards
barely begun letter
those who will not sit at the table any more
look out from picture frames
tears are shining in the candlelight
inside the heart, joy mixes with sadness
carol rocks memories
white wafer waits to be broken
the first star will twinkle in the sky soon
but there are ever more empty chairs around the table

CHRISTMAS TIME

children's voices sound like the bells on a sleigh
time has already come to decorate the Christmas tree
boxes full of decorations, brought by Uncle Adam
and he will be certainly helping kids with them

Anna and Suzanne, George and Walter
with great curiosity, open all boxes, which are
full of the wonders; tinsel decorations,
ballerinas and beautiful wooden horses

the Christmas tree is already standing straight and proud
so fragrant, green with spreading wings around
kids hang the ornaments where they could reach
and so much fun they have with it

there are only the lights and the chain waiting to put on
so proud of their work the children laugh loudly
from the top of the Christmas tree, a little angel looks down
the dog and cat quietly watching it from under the table

now is only to stay patiently waiting to see
what Santa Claus puts for the children under the tree
fulfilling the dreams of those who were well-behaved
or birch is given for these, who were zealous urchins

we'll see pretty soon

Eleni Vasileiou-Asteroskoni
GREECE / GERMANY

Born in Piraeus and of Cretan origin, Eleni is a self-taught painter and poet, and has published two poetry collections, a play and a children's book dedicated to the fight against childhood cancer. In 2016 she was included in volume 28 of the *New Greek Literature*, in 2018 in the *Contemporary Anthology of Modern Greek Poetry* and in 2019 in the *1st Encyclopedia of Modern Greek Writers*. In November 2019 she was awarded by UNESCO Group of Piraeus and Islands for her contribution to Culture, and by the Association of Visual Artists Lanassa for Carriers of Cancer Patients and Other Patients in Greece and Cyprus, for her voluntary work against childhood cancer.

E: eleni-vasiliou@hotmail.com
FB: @ Eleni Vasileiou-Asteroskoni
W: www.asteroskoni.wordpress.com

THIS CHRISTMAS

Once they got going, there was no turning back
all people dancing in the dark
and the Knight oflight they were going again.
Poets and verses that, from kindness to chaos, truly tap into the...
strange hours in the darkness of the year...
I have a voice, I have a dream
but only for you, I have a fear
Life, death, hope, peace
Oh, come in home this Christmas, please...

LITTLE TREE

Little tree
one two three
Look at the balls of stardust in the sky
don't ask me again why
I am dreaming of being out and permitted to shine
and I think of your face, your smile.
Being so alone, don't cry
this Year the angels will fly
and I'll give them all to you to hold
every finger shall have its own ring, gold.
And the song for Fairies I sing
will let smoothly on your hand being
Little tree
one two three...

Seher Hashmi
KINGDOM OF BAHRAIN

Seheris a mummified poet, classified satirist, performer and a podcaster. She lives by the lull of songs, poems and spoken words poetry and often records her rhythmic repertoire via her blog space. Her poetry is inspired by the work of three iconic women, Maya Angelou, Arundhati Roy and Sia Furler. She is an active member of the Bahrain Writers Circle; her work has been published in *Muslim World Today, The Nation*, and in two anthologies of international poets titled T*he Elements* and *Eros.*
E: seherhashmi34@yahoo.com
Instagram: @midnitemusings

STATELESS SPARROW

Out of all that
Hustle bustle of 'who'd reach first'
Incessant jangle of door bells
Curls still hot off iron rollers
Let down in luscious fashion
Endless chitter-chatter,
Uproarious laughter
Hands, one flaunting paisley
Tea cosy cover, other
Pouring out *chai* swirls
In porcelain cups
Hands, Aloe's tender toughness
Insides of Kashmiri pears
Locked in firm embrace
Toffee brown wrinkled knuckles
Dancing on weather-beaten shoulders
Others as if cocoa sheen workers
Playing to the crunch of pine nuts
Shelled for each other
Hands, jingling canoes ferrying
Slightly burnt slices of
Home-made cake
Gone in no time
Leaving many sour-faced
Sheepish smile I wore
Shrinking an inch inwards
Aunties cheeky glares
"How pretty you've grown"
And how Christmas settled in snuggled
Secure in patchwork quilt
Of Jesus will rise
And Prophet's plight
Politicians are failures
So let's stick together
And be there for each other
What has gone missing is a
Stateless sparrow that
Went knitting in and out
All along
Rolling bat eyes at margins
Up and down
Phoenix touch it picked up

Here and there
Houses that dropped
In perfect, borderless
Cross-stitched
*Karez pattern
From *Nani Ammi's handbook
Visible only to those
Who knew how to commune
Without
Syntax, sound, syllables.

NOTES:
*An intricate network of several water inlets for land irrigation, Originated in ancient Persia, still used in Balochistan province of Pakistan.
*Maternal grandmother.

Inspire by *State Bird*, a poem by Ada Limon.

David Dephy
USA / GEORGIA

David is an American/Georgian award-winning poet, novelist, essayist, performer, multimedia artist and painter, and winner of the *Spillwords* Poetry Award, the finalist of the Adelaide Literary Awards for the category of Best Poem. He is named as A Literature Luminary by Bowery Poetry and The Incomparable Poet by Statorec. His works have been published and anthologized in USA, UK and all over the world by the many literary magazines, journals and publishing houses. He lives in New York.
E: dephy21@yahoo.com

SOUND OF CHRISTMAS

We hear a long familiar melody.
Let it sound as gratefulness of our breath.
Shadow falls from our eyes, my love.
Secrets always remain the same.
We do not hear the distant roar of gale, tonight.
We hear that melody; a tide that tugs at us.
The night is calm. Above our heads
a star will flame, again. Time passes
as time does. So much behind us,
and we are not too old at all.
We glare at night and it is so clear
there is never too late for a miracle,
when our eyes touch the night, our lips touch the words
as a secret language of our own breath addressing
a secret world, lifting our bodies to silky night's softness,
we realize how alive we are.

MOTHER EMBRACED HER CHILD

The time is near. The world is ready.
Silence is a mother. She is pregnant
by a word. Heartbeat is a verse.
Breath is a poem. Hope of all mankind.
Along the tarnished echoes, it rolls over us,
rushes by into the streets and windows
where all our stories are retold,
where they carry on deep into the dawning mist.
Glad we are alive, every single morning circled by
premonition of joy. Mother embraced her child
and set him free.

YOU CAN ONLY GO WITH LOVE

They were looking at the stars right there.
Night encircled them. "Escaping from noise
we are still reading between the lines, seeing how
scribble black they are," she said. "Feeling how far
are the stars from earth and anyway, they shine."

"If a story of heaven were true," he asked her.
"Would I become a believer?"
"We can only go with love in this life," she said.
The moon was going down,
sinking under the Queensboro' Bridge.

He thought of all the ideas that maybe he,
or maybe they left undone. He kissed her.
"Time passes as time does," he thought.
"So much behind us," she whispered in his ear.
"Still far to go, what we've left behind as
the moon dips down low," he kissed her again
and the one distant star flew up from the night sky.

Emily Braddock
ENGLAND

Emily speaks Dutch and Portuguese and has travelled extensively, moving to Holland and completing a nursing diploma in 1989, and qualifying as a classical homeopath in 1999. She has worked in Amsterdam, in both nursing and homeopathy, and in Sao Paulo, Brazil, where she taught English as a foreign language. In 2003 she returned to the UK, and now combines working as a cardiac nurse with writing poetry. She is involved in local writing groups and open mic events, has two grown-up children, and lives in North Somerset with her husband.

E: braddockemily@gmail.com

OUR BRIGHTEST STAR

As we near midwinter.

Darkness befriends us, Saturn
Is remembered.
Naked boughs shiver.
Stark in wintry wait
against feeble skies.

When shadow's chill,
Stiffens grass, diamonds
under moonlight.

Voices rise in ritual.
Domine fili unigenite.
Chiming crystal bells
cascade, ringing in layers.
Jesu Christi.

Promise of roast
goose, meaty
gravy red cabbage.
Plum pudding
glowing blue, brandy
butter and cream.
The back door ajar,
To soothe a steamy kitchen.

Bright baubles reflect
in red gold and silver
Rounded contours
of curved walls,
Bowed furnishings.
A snuggle of family,
In crepe paper hats.

A backdrop of evergreen.
Taste of Yule, the rebirth.

Our Brightest Star.

Jill Clark
USA

Jill is from Kansas City, Missouri and now lives in Daytona Beach, Florida. She is a children's poet and freelance writer. Her poetry book *Loose Balloons* for ages 4 -12 published in 2019. Her follow-up book *Where Do Balloons Land?* will be released in 2021 by Taylor and Seale Publishing. Jill is Children's Director at a book publishing house in Daytona Beach, Florida, and conducts kids' activities and lesson plans via Zoom in libraries, schools, museums and other educational institutions in Florida.
E: jillclark2write@gmail.com
E: jillclark2write@twitter.com
W: www.jillswriterscafe.com

THE CHRISTMAS TREE BIRD

The most uncommon common bird to hear
in Northern Christmas climes
is the black-capped chirping chickadee
pitching -
two-note
winter songs.
The trees this small bird sings from,
the conifer, spruce and pine
warm our living rooms and windows
twinkling Love at Christmastime.

Mark Fleisher
USA

Mark is a native of Brooklyn, New York, but now living in Albuquerque, New Mexico. After receiving a journalism degree from Ohio University, Mark worked in Vietnam as an Air Force combat news reporter, and was awarded a Bronze Star. He has published three books of poetry,(with some prose and photography); *Moments of Time, Intersections: Poems from the Crossroads,* and *Reflections: Soundings from the Deep*, in addition to collaborating on a chapbook titled *Obituaries of the Living*. His work has also been published in numerous online and print anthologies in the United States, the United Kingdom, Canada, Kenya, and India. He has also contributed to *Lockdown 2020, War and Battle, On the Road* and *A New World*.
E: markfleisher111@gmail.com
E: markfleisher333@gmail.com

SILENT NIGHT

Christmas Eve
stars still,
moon silent,
wind hushed,
falling snowflakes
almost heard
Tracks of rabbits,
deer, maybe coyote,
embedded without
a whisper
on white blankets

Holiday lights
blurred by stealthy frost
on opaque window panes
all sound suspended
in midnight chill
except for boys and girls
struggling to stay awake
so they may greet Santa
or Saint Nick and their
trove of holiday presents

A HOLIDAY DUET

Grandma Clara celebrated -
recognized is a better word -
Hanukkah and Christmas
in an ecumenical manner,
simply merging them into one
I silently called Chrisukkah

No unwrapping of presents,
no lighting of menorah candles,
no frying of potato latkes,
or spinning of dreidels
nope, Grandma Clara's
Chrisukkah tradition - roast goose

She assumed the identity
of a renown chef,
piercing the bird
so its pools of fat
might be drained
from the roasting pan,
declaring the bird had reached
the desired degree of crispness,
and the gamy meat still moist

Years later, I drained the fat
from the roasting pan, decided
the skin was sufficiently crispy,
and the gamy meat still moist
when my family of mixed faiths
celebrated Chrisukkah

A version of this poem appeared in the author's *Intersections: Poems from the Crossroads* (Mercury HeartLink 2016).

Sarah James
ENGLAND

Editor at V. Press, award-winning poetry and flash fiction imprint, Sarah is a prize-winning poet, fiction writer, journalist and photographer, based in Worcestershire. She is author of seven poetry titles, an Arts Council England funded multimedia hypertext poetry narrative, two novellas and a touring poetry-play. Winner of the CP Aware Award Prize for Poetry 2021, her new collection *Blood Sugar, Sex, Magic* is forthcoming in 2021.
E: lifeislikeacherrytree@yahoo.com
W: www.sarah-james.co.uk

AWAY FROM THE MISTLETOE

The stag on the field's horizon
has a body of muscled heat,
and snow-tipped antlers.

A full-throated robin rests
on the dry stone wall. Song lifts,
drifts, then soars towards the hills.

The barn owl that winged away
from summer's attic nest
hoots from its winter-tree perch.

Near or far, always a sense
of sleek-skied and soft-feathered
creatures watching over us.

The warm mist of each breath
kisses in the Christmas light.

Judy DeCroce
USA

Judy lives and works in upstate New York with her husband poet/artist, Antoni Ooto. Judy is an internationally published poet, flash fiction writer, educator, and avid reader, whose recent works have been published by *Plato's Cave* online, *North of Oxford, The Poet Magazine, Amethyst Review, The Wild Word, The BeZine*, and a number of journals and anthologies. As a professional storyteller and teacher of that genre, she also offers, workshops in flash fiction.
E: judydecroce@yahoo.com
LinkedIn: @judydecroce

OH, CHRISTMAS TREE

Look at you
dressed and ready,
heavier than before,

arms bowed holding memories.

A faithful glitter in darkness,
fragrant green needles
but brittle below your skirt.

December still early,
New Year's Day - a calendar flip away.

Glamour - a poor defence,
          and you, still trying to be merry.

Antoni Ooto
USA

Antoni lives and works in upstate New York with his wife poet/storyteller, Judy DeCroce. Antoni is an internationally published poet and flash fiction writer, as well as being well-known for his abstract expressionist art. He now adds his voice to poetry; reading and studying the works of many poets has opened another means of self-expression. His recent poems have been published in *Amethyst Review, The BeZine, The Poet Magazine, The Active Muse, The Wild Word*, and a number of journals and anthologies.
E: antoniotoart@gmail.com
LinkedIn: @antoniooto

WHITE NOISE

Puddles of galoshes,
boots hugging the door, and
murmurs from the next room

in rising pitches
a chorus in Italian, English
humming with gossip.

A family seasoning the holiday
Thanksgiving, Christmas...

voices at a table arm-to-arm
a dozen conversations
knotted one-to-one

lulling the half-asleep child
on a daybed
heaped with coats.

Tracy Davidson
ENGLAND

Tracy lives in Warwickshire, and writes poetry and flash fiction. Her work has appeared in various publications and anthologies, including: *Poet's Market, Writing Magazine, Mslexia, Atlas Poetica, Modern Haiku, The Binnacle, A Hundred Gourds, Shooter, Artificium, Journey to Crone, The Great Gatsby Anthology, WAR, In Protest: 150 Poems for Human Rights* and others.

E: james0309@btinternet.com

WHAT THE DONKEY SAW

I was peacefully dreaming
on a cold and silent night,
when a woman started screaming
and gave me quite a fright.

A kindly looking stranger
led a woman through the door,
he emptied out my manger,
placed my food upon the floor.

The sound of muttered praying
and the look upon her face
prevented me from braying
at this invasion of my space.

She really was a beauty
and though I can't explain,
somehow I knew it was my duty
to see her through the pain.

I looked into her gentle eyes,
she met my loving stare,
it seemed to calm her painful cries
to have me standing there.

In the middle of the night,
on a blanket I'd once worn,
I stood and watched the magic sight
as a baby boy was born.

People came to see the child
as he lay on his makeshift bed.
He never cried, was meek and mild
as all touched his little head.

In a stable, among the straw,
where this lowly donkey stood,
my heart tells me what I saw
was the start of something good.

CHRISTMAS DAY

children wake early
gasp in wonder at stockings
bulging with presents
happy laughter fills the house
loved ones gather together

huge piles of paper
I wonder why I bothered
with fancy gift wrap
and wince as I remember
I forgot the batteries

after the Queen's speech
my husband carves the turkey
we wear paper hats
tell each other silly jokes
heard a hundred times before

full of Christmas pud
my father snores in his chair
we shush the children
who argue over whose turn
it is for the washing up

at night we curl up
by the fire, eating mince pies
watching 'Doctor Who'
as he battles to save Earth
from evil grinning snowmen

tears before bedtime -
one toy already broken -
sleep beckons us all
another Christmas over
we look forward to New Year

Máire Malone
ENGLAND / REPUBLIC OF IRELAND

Máire was born and reared in Dublin where she worked as a medical secretary. She moved to the UK, studied Arts and Psychology, and followed a career in Counselling & Psychotherapy. Several of her poems have been selected and published by Ver Poets and other anthologies. She has had short story prize wins in *Scribble* magazine, and a story was shortlisted in Words and Women Competition, 2018. She was selected for a place on the Novel Studio Course in 2017, where she completed a draft of her debut novel, *The Dream Circle*. Her novel has been selected as a Finalist in Eyelands International Book Awards 2019, and *The Irish Echo*, New York, published an essay about it earlier this year. She lives in Hertfordshire with her husband.
E: maireowens@aol.com
W: www.mairemalone.com

CHRISTMAS SWANKS

My father made up bedtime tales
Of banqueting and feasts
Smacking his lips between each course
He catalogued the menu -
Plates of ham, turkey roast and spuds -
Chocolate, as much as you could eat
We drooled until our bellies ached.

No golden coach transported us to palace balls
No fancy books to illustrate the story-line
But as we watched the embers in our bedroom grate,
His words inflamed our senses into pageantry
We were Swanks swishing in the sheerest silk
Our white gloved hands outstretched
Hair, spring curling at the merest touch

When my father had dethroned
Retreated to his lesser world, we ate –
The turkey tasted succulent
The chocolate so sweet

Nivedita Karthik
INDIA

Nivedita is a graduate in Immunology from the University of Oxford. She currently resides in Gurgaon, India, and works as a science and medical editor/reviewer. She is an accomplished Bharatanatyam dancer and published poet. She also loves writing stories. Her poetry has appeared in *Glomag, The Society of Classical Poets, The Epoch Times, The Bamboo Hut, and Eskimopie* and is forthcoming in The *Sequoyah Cherokee River Journal*.
E: nivedita5.karthik@gmail.com
Blog: www.justrandomwithnk.com

CHRISTMAS YEAR-ROUND

The most joyous season of the year is here!
Christmas! It comes just once a year

During Christmas all the lights burn brighter
and the hugs get a little longer and tighter

The streets are filled with cheery shoppers
buying presents and polka-dotted Christmas poppers

Church roofs are dotted with a sprinkling of snow
and the warm fireplace emanates a golden glow

Christmastime comes but once a year
spreading joy and happiness and good cheer.

But the spirit of Christmas should last longer than a day
since the giving, sharing, and loving never fade away.

RECIPE FOR THE PERFECT CHRISTMAS

The ingredients are not too hard to find.
But search not in a store or the pantry,
look inside you and you shall see
the perfect Christmas recipe.

Start off with some childlike optimism and wonder.
Pour in a splash of laughter and good cheer
        and add in a heaping spoonful of gratefulness.
Mix well with some tender loving care.
Gather all the appreciation and
        toss out the frustrations and sorrows
It's now time to stir in the goodness of love
        to dispel the away the fumes of daily despair.
Whisk in some kindness and lots of hugs
        and sprinkle some giggles of joy...
And we're done!

Last, but certainly not least,
Feel the warm golden glow pervade
                        This is the spirit of Christmas.

Russell Willis
USA

Ethicist and online education entrepreneur, Russell emerged as a poet in 2019. Since then, his poetry has been published (or accepted for publication) in *Breathe, Peeking Cat, Le Merle, As Above So Below, Grand Little Things, Frost Meadow Review's Pandemic Poetry, October Hill, Cathexis Northwest, Meat for Tea, The MOON magazine, Snapdragon: A Journal of Art & Healing, Tiny Seed Literary Journal, The Esthetic Apostle*, and three anthologies. Russell grew up in and around Texas, was vocationally scattered throughout the Southwest and Great Plains for many years, and is now settled in Vermont, with his wife, Dawn.
E: willisdrr63@gmail.com
W: www.REWilisWrites.com

SO, SO SMALL

So, so small, are you aware
"You will wear your name so well"?
"You will make your Father proud!"
This she whispered in his ear.

So, so small, are you aware
Of all that goes around you;
The comings and the goings,
Expectations, hopes, and fears?

So, so small, are you aware
As your eyes peer into mine
That I love you little one
Precious gift not just to me?

So, so small, are you aware
The promise you embody
Love incarnate will be known
In the man that you will be?

So, so small, are you aware
Even now I will give you
To a world in need of peace
To a world that's seeking joy?

So, so small, are you aware
On your birthday you're the gift
You the blessing angels sing
You, my darling little boy?

STARLIGHT

In the starlight
      a baby murmurs
      a mother whispers
      a father sighs
Drawn by the starlight
      shepherds gather
      wise ones ponder
      angels delight
Soon comes the dawn-light
      the gift has been given
      a new light shines bright
      may your life shine with this light

CHRISTMAS SKY

Is the Christmas sky
the brilliant night
the host of stars
illuminating paths for
curious souls
and a venue for celestial song?

Or is the Christmas Sky
the dawn that greets
a baby's cry, a mother's sigh
the not yet blue
no longer black
too early to tell if
cloud or refracted light
on the canopy of life
that not yet time
before the gift of a
new day is opened?

Laurinda Lind
USA

Laurinda lives so far north in New York State that she only misses being Canadian by a few miles. Some publications / acceptances are in *Amsterdam Quarterly, Antithesis Journal, BlueHouse Journal, Compose, Crannóg, Earthen Lamp Journal, Here Comes Everyone, Spillway, Two Thirds North*, and *With Painted Words*; also in anthologies *Visiting Bob: Poems Inspired by the Life and Work of Bob Dylan* (New Rivers Press) and *AFTERMATH: Explorations of Loss and Grief* (Radix Media).
E: writers@ridgeviewtel.us

KEEP IT HANDY OVERHEAD

Mistletoe, a semi-parasitic plant
good for more than the ambush
kiss, could cure your nerves
and your sleepless nights. Two
teaspoons in a hot cup could
even mend the metronome
swinging madly in your chest,
Merry Christmas. But use
the European kind called
viscus album, anything
else isn't safe, and don't take
it raw, either. Just like all else
alive in the coldest cold, its
berries that ripen in December,
its green despite the snow, it
helps you rejoice in the miracle
that is your life. You might
as well lean in for the kiss.

Deepika Singh
INDIA

Deepika hails from Margherita-Assam. A teacher by profession, poetry is an undying passion for her; through poetry she explores herself. Considering self-satisfaction as a vision; she loves to utter the unsaid word. Some of her work has been featured in national and international platforms, and is the first female from the Eastern part of India to make a State and World Record in Rangoli. She believes that words can change the world if put in a right way, and through poetry she hopes to touch people's soul.
E: dipikamajm@gmail.com

BELLS OF JOY

The sky is pink and red
Ah! A colourful ambience.
Irrespective of their religion
Folks assembled to the tune of carols.
The merry giggling sound of kids
Feels like utopia.
Miles away from pain,
Far-flung from hatred,
There is only one religion,
And the religion is of Humanity.
Let this Christmas brighten a gloomy house,
Give relief to indigence,
Warmth to a lonely granny.
Shelter for orphans.
Books to enlighten.
No war only peace.
Let this Christmas we shed away the beast inside us.
And be like Santa spreading the fragrance of happiness.
Oh! Dear folks then only our lord will be pleased
Let this serenity prevail.

Anthony Ward
ENGLAND

Anthony tries his best not to write but he just can't help himself. He writes in order to rid himself and lay his thoughts to rest. He derives most of his inspiration from listening to Classical Music and Jazz, since it is often the mood which invokes him. He has recently been published in *Streetcake, Bluepepper, Shot Glass Journal, Mad Swirl* and *Flash Fiction North.*
E: wardanthony301@outlook.com

CHRISTMAS

O, how I embellish those early hibernal afternoons
Between the hours of three and four
When all seems quieter and serene.
The lowing sun receding with warmth
As you pass the fairy lights hanging from conifers
That confine the village into a community.
Where you can smell Christmas in the air,
Feel the atmosphere imbibing.
Refining the sentiments of the past with childhood revivification.

The first snowflakes of the year fall in perfect symmetry,
Resting softly on the ground,
While the wind whistles through the door and you hold on for your
dear wife,
Serenaded by frabjous carol singers
Adding to the sonorous silence.
The spruce spruced in tender presence,
In typical tradition.

Christmas is a timeless age,
When family and friends gather together for festive fun
With celebrations, tribulations and salutations,
Before resuming conversations unfinished from the year before,
Lost for the past eleven months.

Dr. Sarah Clark
KINGDOM OF BAHRAIN

Sarah is from the UK and has lived in the Middle East since 2006. Her poems have featured in three anthologies of *The Poet Magazine, Suicide, Lockdown 2020* and *A New World*. She is also the Principal Writer for the travel series *101 Things to See and Do*. Sarah is the Founder of the Baloo's Buddies in Bahrain - a non-profit program using pet dogs to enhance the life and social skills of children of all abilities with communication difficulties. When not working on large scale inclusive projects, Sarah enjoys writing in a variety of formats including children's literature and poetry. Writing primarily on themes of inclusion, mental health and the environment, Sarah's poems and artwork has been featured in a number of poetry events and exhibitions in Bahrain since 2018.
E: sarah@dscwll.com
FB: @Baloosbuddies
FB: @@sarahclarke888

THE CHRISTMAS PUZZLE

As a child I never knew
That Christmas didn't always have snow
And turkey wasn't on everyone's table
While others waited 'til midnight to glow

I never knew that crackers didn't pop everywhere
And some homes had a silver tree
That Santa had different places to go
What you mean he didn't come just for me?

I never knew how our tree appeared on the Eve
Not like now sometimes weeks before
As I ran in the lounge on Christmas morn',
My eyes popping in awe

I never knew that some didn't have plenty
That gifts might be in short supply
Or that others didn't celebrate the same
And the festival might pass them by

I never knew why we sang many carols
We weren't such a religious lot
I guess it was fun to belt them out
As we all did during the Christmas slot

I always knew that on this day
We would fill our house with guests
And I'd shuffle around with trays of food
While decked out in my Sunday best

I always knew Aunty Flo' would be there
Begging us all music to play
And one by one our tunes we'd perform,
Encores seeming to last all day

I always knew there'd be endless questions
From people I hardly knew
All asking for facts on this and that
Their knowledge banks happily to renew

I always knew we'd eat too much
Crack jokes, play games all day

It was part of our ritual every year
Oh how we wished Santa would stay!

But I always knew, if the truth be told
That Christmas would be soon in bags
And twelve days later all in a heap
With only "Do your thank you note!" nags!

John Tunaley
ENGLAND

Born in Manchester, England in 1945 (father; foundry hand, mother; crane-driver), John now lives in Robin Hoods' Bay, North Yorkshire. He's in a few writing groups plus a painting group... a tai-chi group... a music group... his French class... then there's Open Gardens to help sort out for every June (proceeds to the Alzheimer's Society), and the grandchildren who demand he plays with them... he gets no rest. He enjoys the 'anthology' approach, and tends to stick to sonnets as the form exercises some control over his worse excesses.
E: johntunaley@yahoo.co.uk

SIX WISE PEOPLE

Two wise men and one wise woman took it
Into their heads to visit us today.
Robin came on his trusty bicycle,
But only from Hayburn Wyke where he'd left
His truck. He had to pedal back to it
In the dark. Wisely, he had a head-lamp.
Steve and Ruth walked the hundred metres or
So from where they live. Sue, Anne and I shared
A drink and exchanged Christmas cards with them.
Laughter played its' part, as did chat about
Folks various medical conditions.
"It's being so cheerful keeps us going"
I offered. In our wisdom we moved on
To discuss Boxing Day organ concerts...

Robin Hood's Bay, 23/12/2018

THE ORGAN

A pile of stones stands silent and uncast,
The choir sounds touchingly irresolute
Searching for the carol's last falling line.
When they stop, I go in and creep upstairs...
It's warmer outside! Voice and violin
Reach out from the frigid interior
To where the striped umbrella outstared me.

In its ocean of mist, this island church
Is a cold flint awaiting steel-struck sparks.
I nurse my, by now, half-bottle of red
As the organist's pitter-pattering
Pedalling far outstrips the tunes slow notes.

Moisture from mulled wine and singing condenses,
As people pack up and leaving commences.

St. Stephen's Day, Old Church of St Stephen, Robin Hood's Bay, 26/12/2015.

Gerri Leen
USA

Gerri is a Rhysling-nominated poet from Northern Virginia. She has poetry published in: *Eye to the Telescope, Star*Line, Dreams & Nightmares, Songs of Eretz, Polu Texni, NewMyths.com, Neo-Opsis* and others. She also writes fiction in many genres (as Gerri Leen for speculative and mainstream, and Kim Strattford for romance) and is a member of HWA and SFWA.
E: gerrileen@gerrileen.com
W: www.gerrileen.com

DRESSED IN HOLIDAY STYLE

Airplane travel, holiday mania
People stuffing presents in overhead
Bins nowhere near their seats
Pre 9/11, when luggage was a free-for-all
Carry-on limits? Who paid attention?
My presents are long since mailed home
Bouncing along on a UPS truck
I follow in the plane, crammed into a
Window seat, my row-mate asking if he can
Stow a bag under the seat in front of me
It's a five-hour flight, more if the winds
Are against us
But it's Christmas, so I let him
And try to find a home for my feet
In the small space left

Finally home, flying in, Mount Rainier
A glistening welcome
There are mountains in Virginia
But nothing like this
We land and my parents are waiting
My mother has her "Where's my little girl?"
Expression on, my father's more serene
But he's just driven sixty miles
On roads that look clear but might not be
He's probably glad to have a break
From trying to spot black ice
As well as see his daughter

When we get home, the house is the same
Three thousand miles and fifteen months
And nothing has changed
The nativity scene sits on sparkly cotton atop the TV
The artificial tree stands tall, same gold lights, same spiral
Garland in gold, too, strands and strands of it
The balls my mom once spent a whole year making
Foam orbs covered with velvet and beads and ribbon
Mixed with older glass ornaments
Presents under the tree, the ones I sent, too
UPS comes through again

Christmas has a smell but not evergreen since the

Tree is plastic and metal
Not bayberry or cranberry, since my mom
And aunt are allergic to scented candles
But the smell of cider, spiced and hot
Of pumpkin pie baking in the oven
Of teriyaki wings, our Christmas Eve tradition
Soon there will be turkey cooking
A spiral-cut ham will start off the day
Along with scrambled eggs and sweet rolls
And more cider, the scent of spiced apples

Presents are opened between breakfast and dinner
All that work buying them and they are ripped apart
Like piranha on an unsuspecting cow
Cries of "Thank you" from all over the room
My brothers and their wives here, my nephews, too
Sometimes someone brings a guest who finds themself
Caught up gift-less in the present frenzy
With a family that kisses on the lips and still says grace
Only Dad forgets who everyone is when he asks God to
Bless us by name — it's a family joke how forgetful he is
My brothers and I snicker trying to keep the silliness
On simmer

Too soon it is over, Christmas and then the days after, and then
Back to the airport, now-unwrapped presents
Are shoved into crammed overheads
The flight attendants urge us to our seats
Full plane today, it was packed coming out, too
Who knew Seattle to D.C. would be so popular?
My row-mate wants to use the space under
The seat in front of me for his stuff
I'm headed back East, leaving my family
Christmas is over, New Years lacks the same
Generosity, no brotherly love overcomes me
As I smile but say, "No"

THE FIRST CHRISTMAS AFTER

Stores shine red and gold and green
But you see in shades of grey
Songs ring out — you're so tired of them
But silence only reminds you
That you're alone

You used to love the holiday
You may love it again
But not this year — not when you've lost so much
It's all right to be sad, all right to cry
When you're alone

People you love try to hold you
You slip like water through their fingers
Loss is like that: makes you nimble
Makes joy seem far away
It will creep back

Forget the Yuletide sentiments
Forget the malls and the carols
Look for the ones who love you
They are there
Waiting for you

You're not alone

Margaret Clifford
AUSTRALIA

Margaret is a Brisbane poet who began writing after her retirement from full time work as an educator. She has published two collections, *Stitched Pages* in 2016 and *Layers of Life* in 2019. Many of her poems are used as reflections in rituals and community gatherings, and have been published in local journals and magazines. Several of her poems have been published in *A Collection of Poetry and Prose*.

E: mdkanga@gmail.com

PRESENCE

A child is born!
There she lies

in her mother's arms
firmly wrapped

a wondrous gift
glowing with love

radiating innocence
breathtakingly beautiful!

At Christmas
our hearts know

and leap for joy
at this pure love

permeating
our world

beaming through
a newborn child.

Cathy Cade

ENGLAND

Cathy is a retired librarian who sometimes lives with her husband and dogs in Cambridgeshire's Fenland surrounded by fields. The rest of the time they live across the fence from London's Epping Forest. Her writing has been published in Scribble, *Tales of the Forest, Flash Fiction Magazine, To Hull and Back Short Story Anthology 2018*, and The Poet's *On the Road*. Her verses owe more to Pam Ayres than Poe or Plath. Her stories have been placed third in three competitions, shortlisted in four others and longlisted by the National Literacy Trust. Her books include: *A Year Before Christmas, The Godmother* (a retelling of Cinderella's story) and *Witch Way, and other ambiguous stories.*

E: cathincade@gmail.com
W: www.cathy-cade.com
FB: @cathycade.wordsmith
Goodreads: @cathycade
Smashwords: @cathincade

CHRISTMAS WRAPPING

While one hand holds the paper,
other groping for the tape, her
goodwill fades as sticky tape escapes her lurches.
She lets go the gift, to travel
to the tape that caused the hassle
and the perfect wrap unravels.
Curses!

Christmas present trapping
while the other side's unwrapping
and the tape is strapping fingers to the box,
is a skill she's never mastered.
Disaster! She's plastered the label to the table.
Hubby mocks.

But he won't wield the scissors
to help her do the business.
And as weeks fly by to Christmas, pressures rise
to wrap every festive offering
for her children and their offspring
—whether fake bling or the real thing—by yuletide.

When they're stacked under the tree,
looking higgly piggledy,
and the grandkids come to see
and anticipate with glee, tree-lights winter-twinkling.
They won't go in Santa's sack
because the corners come unwrapped,
but it's worth her aching back
when her grandchildren feedback: Gran's look... interesting.

A YEAR BEFORE CHRISTMAS

'Twas the night before Christmas when Santa's new elf,
in the vast, silent workshop, sat all by herself.
She'd been fetching and carrying, sent to and fro
making tea, running errands – the least of the low.

And she'd mucked out the stables, not noticing that
daft old Rudolph was munching her new elven hat.
So it was, that when Santa Claus marshalled the rest,
Emmie failed to pass muster – improperly dressed.

As the sleigh jingled off through the wintery skies,
Em recalled seeing oversized dark dragonflies
every day, as she shovelled snow, cold and downcast.
She'd heard them approach, and she'd watched them drone past.

Metal mules don't need feeding or stalls mucking out.
She envisaged a prototype – drafted it out.
And, because Emmie Elf was a born engineer,
it was ready for testing soon after New Year.

When old Santa awoke from his post-Christmas nap
– around Easter – he heard an insistent tap-tap.
He threw open his door, and the drone that was knocking
flew in, to deliver a filled Christmas stocking.

Santa welcomed technology – no luddite, he.
He went over Em's drawings with thinly veiled glee.
His eyes were a-twinkle, his morning smile, gappy.
'Give 'em antlers, to keep the traditionalists happy.'

'With a flight deck controlling them all from the sleigh,
we could beta-test next week – perhaps Saturday.'
The older elves muttered, though younger ones cheered,
and some glitches occurred as the doubters had feared.

Busy months hurried past until summer was gone.
Father Christmas pushed Emmie to move things along,
till, at last, Santa's sleigh had its instrumentation.
The elves shuffled out for the grand demonstration.

One took off and crash-dived, and two flew away,
and one was attacked by a large bird of prey.

A couple collided, and one hit the wall,
and some couldn't pull up their stockings at all.

While, it's true, some delivered their load as directed,
still, more work was needed before 'twas perfected.
The younger, brash elven-folk jeered, and they laughed,
while the older ones claimed the whole idea was daft.

The concept was fantasy, science fiction, crass...
''Cos you can't replace reindeer, and Emmie's a lass.'
Angry more with themselves for beginning to dream
of a cushier Christmas with Emmie's bold scheme.

But Santa smiled kindly and smothered a chuckle.
''Twere worth trying, lass.' Then he tightened his buckle.
December was on them. While Em tweaked her coding,
the others were sorting and packing and loading.

The adverts and streetlights and windows of shops
were a-glitter with tinsel and other Yule props.
And newer elves tidied and swept, and made tea,
in keen anticipation of Christmas to be.

'Twas the night before Christmas, when children in bed
had no inkling of Santa's sleigh parked overhead,
as the elves filled the skies on their winged, metal steeds,
with brass antlers to steer them at dizzying speeds.

Old St. Nick and the reindeer could rest their tired feet
While the elf-guided drones made their drops in each street.
Then, trailing like stardust, they followed the sleigh,
Wishing, peace, health and laughter to all on their way.

Bernadette Perez

USA

Bernadette is based in Belen, New Mexico. In 1990 she received the Silver Poet Award from *World of Poetry*. Published in over 100 publications between 2015-2019, her work has appeared in *The Wishing Well; Musings, Small Canyons* anthology, *Poems 4 Peace, Contribution to La Familia: La Casa de Colores,* and may others. She was also included in the mega-unity poem by Juan Felipe and *The Americans Museum Inscription* by Shinpei Takeda.

E: bpburritos@aol.com

GIVE

Give with all your heart
Give unconditionally
Give without explanation
Give without expecting anything in return
Give without details
Give with no regrets
Give just to Give

Hussein Habasch
KURDISTAN / GERMANY

Hussein Habasch is a poet from Afrin, Kurdistan. He currently lives in Bonn, Germany. His poems have been translated into English, German, Spanish, French, Chinese, Turkish, Persian, Albanian, Uzbek, Russian, Italian, Bulgarian, Lithuanian, Hungarian, Macedonian, Serbian, Polish and Romanian, and has had his poetry published in a large number of international anthologies. His books include: *Drowning in Roses, Fugitives across Evros River, Higher than Desire and more Delicious than the Gazelle's Flank, Delusions to Salim Barakat, A Flying Angel, No pasarán* (in Spanish), *Copaci Cu Chef* (in Romanian), *Dos Árboles and Tiempos de Guerra* (in Spanish), *Fever of Quince* (in Kurdish), *Peace for Afrin, peace for Kurdistan* (in English and Spanish), *The Red Snow* (in Chinese), *Dead arguing in the corridors* (in Arabic) and *Drunken trees* (in Kurdish). He participated in many international festivals of poetry including: Colombia, Nicaragua, France, Puerto Rico, Mexico, Germany, Romania, Lithuania, Morocco, Ecuador, El Salvador, Kosovo, Macedonia, Costa Rica, Slovenia, China, Taiwan and New York City.
E: habasch70@hotmail.com

THE SAXOPHONE PLAYER

As a gift in a busy city
He stood under the Christmas tree
And played his saxophone
With a great mastery.
He wasn't a famous musician like
Sonny Rollins,
Coleman Hawkins,
Lester Young
Or Joe Henderson.
He played without chorus,
Chanters or choir...
The echo of his eternal playing
Was carried by the street,
Conveying it to the hearts
Of passers-by without permission.
He was neither ambitious nor willing,
Except to collect some money.
Maybe he'd buy bread,
Cigarettes,
Or a bottle of wine.
Maybe he'd buy a small gift
And give it on Christmas to his little daughter.
Next week I will remember the saxophone player
And I will tell him in secret:
MERRY CHRISTMAS, great musician!

Lovelle Sumayang
PHILIPPINES

Lovelle is a creative literary artist, poetess, a passionate writer of free poetry, essays and stories. She's a founder of Creative Writing For Everyone, and moderator of the writers' platform DEMO GOG.
E: love.sumayang@gmail.com

CHRISTMAS GLITTER
Translated into English - Kabishev A. K.

"Our House, only small"
It's not that beautiful
But when is something really shines,
You will want watch, follow lines.

Light, oh, so tasty!
Take a look at the glimmer
A Christmas winking,
Definitely, you'll keep on beholding.

THE SOUND OF JOY IN HOLIDAY SEASON
Translated into English - Kabishev A. K.

Here's the sound of joyful noise,
The sound of much excitement,
Hear the most wonderful voice,
Singing in lovely moment.

The tears of gladness in heart,
Rhymes in music of the lyre,
Come, let good harmony start,
As the love song burn with fire.

Hear the sound of joyful voice!
Hear the music as we rejoice!
Let's celebrate this lovely season!
Be filled with gladness despite all reason.

William Khalipwina Mpina
MALAWI

William is a Malawian poet, fiction writer, essayist, economist and teacher. His writing reflects on the mundane and the everyday. A co-editor of *Walking the Battlefield* a bilingual collection of verse on the theme of hope during the Covid-19 pandemic, and editor of *Tilembe Newsletter*, a brainchild of Malawi Union for Academic and Non-fiction Authors, Mpina has works in online international literary magazines such as K*alahari Review, Literary Shanghai, Writers Space Africa, African writer, Nthanda review, Scribble Publication, Atunis Poetry, Author-me, Poetica and Expound, Brave World Magazine*; and in over ten local and international anthologies including; *LOCKDOWN 2020, On The Road* and *Writing robotics: Africa versus Asia*. His books include *Princess from the Moon* (2020), *Shattered Dreams* (2019), *Blood Suckers* (2019), *Shadows of Death and other poems* (2016), *Namayeni* (2009) and *Njiru* (2003).
E: williammpina3@gmail.com
FB: @William.Mpina

PORTRAIT OF CHRISTMAS

same same
same time
same same
every year
merriful moments
slaughtering
& gathering
dancing
& drinking
& forgetting
Whose birthday
songs skirting around
beef, sausages and
the joyful braii stand
& untitled fights
celebrate Bethlehem
everyone a child
of God -
By feathering
smoke with sweets
& flying it
through the windows
fog of celebration
in the slums
staring at the horizon
sozzled with heat
Life is thus
In my Lunzu town
come December 25.

WHEN THE YEAR'S SOUL SINGS

when the year's soul sings
the price of sacrifice
proud birds circle around it
the lesson is learnt
the roof cannot hold itself
the pestle cannot grind grain
without reinforcement
salvation of mankind
wind laughs as it beats
drums of liberation
for Christ the mediator
every year sweetening Christmas.

Stella Peg Carruthers
NEW ZEALAND

Stella Peg Carruthers is an emerging writer from Aotearoa. Born and bred in the capital city of Wellington or Poneke, she still lives there and is employed as a library assistant at an academic library as well as working in community work and running her own freelance writing business. She is currently working on her debut novel, a cross-genre family saga about the power of literature to change lives. She has found publishing success both internationally and within New Zealand. Her poems have been published in online and print publications, and she has been long listed for a number of short story competitions. She has two mental health themed personal essay's due for publication in anthologies to be released in 2021. She writes reviews regularly for the New Zealand Poetry Society. As well as writing, she facilitates a writer's group in her home city and has in the past co-presented writing based self-development workshops for women. A keen plant-based cook, Stella also loves walking, yoga, music and knitting. Additionally, she runs sustainable living workshops at her local community education centre to support lifelong learning principles.

E: stellacarr20@gmail.com
Blog: www.geographichearts.blog

MISTLETOE

Tinsel hangs in nooses.
The trees are already dying to brown.

Paper is ripped to pieces and trodden
through a house that bangs with
glass bowls in the sink and voices
hushed to raise on the front step.

I try to fold paper into squares.
Think I'll use it next year maybe.

With smiling men in my hands I step
through the wreathed doorway.

Santa kisses my palms.

TO WORSHIP A DIFFERENT SORT OF CHRIST

To the receptionist on the first floor Christmas has come early.
Ready for the Big Day three weeks early she has hung
Golden tinsel and empty boxes are be-ribboned
at the foot of her desk.
Stars fall down around her.

Every morning through afternoon she observes people
clambering up and down the narrow stairs.
They wear faded shirts and paint splashed jeans.
They carry canvases.
Blank on the journey up.
Coloured on the way down.
All of us are Elves in workshops on the floors above.
The bells rung; are ones we shake ourselves.
Our songs peal over rooftop in visionary chants.
And we have changed the light bulb in Rudolph's nose.
It now shines white, not the warning of red.

As for Santa.
He is stuck between floors.
We knew the lift was old.
The doors warped and metal slid.
There is often a sound as we carry down a new series.

We pass it off on the rumble of passing trolley bus
Or the blast of music from the studios above.
We do not pause.
You do not stop with an ocean balanced
on your shoulders.

John Grey
USA / AUSTRALIA

John is an Australian poet, US resident, recently published in *New World Writing, Dalhousie Review* and *Connecticut River Review*. Work upcoming in *Hollins Critic, Redactions* and *California Quarterly*.
E: jgrey5790@gmail.com

DRUMMER BOY

What's the noise
emanating from the bedroom?
How could I forget.
It's the drum kit

I bought him for Christmas.
My wife says every child
should learn a musical instrument.
That crash of cymbals,

thump of snare,
is my wife getting it wrong.
And yes it's better this
than him roaming the streets

with the kind of kids we've
always warned about.
But if only we could have
afforded a piano.

But, then again,
who wants to hear
Chopin being mangled
morning, noon and night.

And actually, for
all the noise,
no question he has
a sense of rhythm.

And I won't be telling him
to stop any time soon.
Not while my heart's still beating.
Like a drum so they tell me.

Peter H. Dietrich
BULGARIA / UK

Originally from the UK, and after travelling the world non-stop for over 40 years as freelance reporter/film-maker, writing non-stop all the way and in various forms, Peter has paused to try to see some of his more personal writings read and published. A number of his poems have been published in literary magazines worldwide, and currently he is working on two musicals; one a comedy, the other a tragedy - the musical-comedy has also been published as a children's storybook, with original illustrations. Peter has also self-published two volumes of poetry; *Forty Days & Forty Nights* and *Inbetween Before And After.*
E: awwcinc@yahoo.co.uk

WINTERY LANDSCAPE

Wintery landscape, wintery blues,
Go pull on your favourite shoes,
Let's plant footprints deep in the snow,
Running hand in hand as the cold nights glow,
We'll skip along to old Jack Frost's tune,
While singing praises to the silvery moon,
And as the countless flakes fall glistening from above
We'll melt them one by one with our shining love.

Wintery landscape, wintery dreams,
Go dig out all your favourite themes,
Let's throw snowballs without any rules,
Then warm the cockles of our hearts beside the blazing Yules,
Old Santa is flying by with his trusty reindeer,
The kids all go rushing out to grab some good cheer,
And when the stars are twinkling in the dark sky up above
We'll capture them and pin them to our ever-glowing love.

Wintery landscape, wintery trees,
Go grab the ring with the jangling keys,
Let's open the hearts of all the sleeping flowers,
And rescue the lonely damsels from their ivory towers,
Then we'll hurry on to unlock every solid door,
Behind which the lonely hearts are crying out for more,
And when the tears and smiles are all gathered up above
We'll drink them as a warming toast to our beloved love.

Wintery landscape, wintery world,
Go stoke the fire where the old cat is curled,
Let's raid the kitchen for the freshly baked mince-pies,
Then reap all the goodness from our mother's knowing eyes,
The carol singers ring and serenade the silent night,
While the mulled wine is steaming to put the whole world right,
And when our deepest wishes are all floating up above
We'll let them go and watch them as they carry off our love.

Wintery landscape, wintery blues,
Go take the gifts to those who cannot choose,
Let's tell the magic story to those who want to hear,
Then count the booming chimes that ring in the brand new year,
Warm kisses in the winter cost nothing to give or take,
And hugging distant family relieves the long heartache,

So when the cold comes creeping in from somewhere up above,
We'll warm the wintery world again with our eternal love.

Yash Seyedbagheri
USA

Yash is a graduate of Colorado State University's MFA program. His stories, *Soon, How To Be A Good Episcopalian* and *Tales From A Communion Line*, were nominated for Pushcarts. Yash's work has been published in *The Journal of Compressed Creative Arts, Write City Magazine*, and *Ariel Chart*, among others.
E: kaiseryash@gmail.com

LIGHT

red and green lights flicker
white and blues ones too
festooned from rooftops
from Christmas trees
and porches
a torchlight parade
bathing the shimmering snow
and the shadows of passers-by
on a December's eve
welcome, they whisper
weary smiles widening

WINTER'S DANCE

Nutcracker marches
the sugar plum fairies dance
it's hard to not join them
in the snowbanks
to pirouette with the lights flickering
and a deep December's dusk falling
lavender, pink, and pale wintry blue
the shadows wink

Eva Petropoulou-Lianoy
GREECE

Eva loved journalism and in 1994 went to France to work as a journalist for the French newspaper *Le Libre Journal*. However, her love for Greece won over, and she returned to live and work in Athens. Eva has written a number of books in French including; *Géraldine et le lutin du lac*, which was subsequently translated into Greek, approved by the Ministry of Education, and turned into a theatre play performed in schools around the country and abroad. In Greece, she published *The Daughter of the Moon*, which contained 80 illustrations by acclaimed artist Mr. Hristo Mavref, using 35 different shades of blue and pink. The following years she published five more books for children. Her recent book *Travel with Fairytales of Lafcadio Patrick Hearn, myths and stories from the Far East*, was illustrated by well-known Greek sculptor and artist Mrs. Ntina Anastasiadou.
E: Eviepara@yahoo.fr
FB: @evapetropoylou.lianosii

CHRISTMAS

I hear the bells
Angels hurry up and fly high
Follow the big star that shine
Lord is born
Alleluia

I hear the bells
Children are singing and laughing
Hope is rise
Lord is born
Alleluia

I hear the bells
The dark will disappear
The sun is here
Pray with all your strength
Lord is born
Alleluia

CHRISTMAS IS COMING

The season of gifts and family union
I miss the time that I was a little child
I was with grandmother
She make Christmas so special
Lights everywhere in her home
Smells of cookies
And pancakes

Christmas we feel them first deeply in our heart
The time to forgive and say sorry has come
Open heart and write down to a paper the names of all that persons
that might hurt you

Christmas coming
Mysterious things will guide us
Make a wish.
Believe strongly
And Peace will come again

Christmas coming
Lord Jesus will born
A new self will come out

Mike Wilson
USA

Mike's work has appeared in magazines including *Cagibi Literary Journal, Stoneboat, The Aurorean*, and *The Ocotillo Review*, and in his book *Arranging Deck Chairs on the Titanic* (Rabbit House Press, 2020), political poetry for a post-truth world. Mike resides in Central Kentucky.

E: mikewilsonauthor@earthlink.net
W: www.mikewilsonwriter.com
FB: @mikewilsonauthor
Instagram: @mikewilsonauthor
Twitter: @mikewilsonauth1

WE LEAVE THE LIGHTS ON

I rise in darkness of the unformed day
drift to our living room, where my hand
reaching for the light switch is arrested
by the sight of Christmas tree lights –
blue and red, purple, yellow, green,
a burning cone of silent stars steering
hope past shoals we cannot see
in these strange seas of uncertainty
to what we need this Christmas to be

CHRISTMAS WITH FAMILY

A Disney movie plays, a holograph
projected against a screen of dust motes
hanging in the air like COVID-19
My wife is bored. I say it's almost over
and it's good if you haven't seen it before
When the credits roll, I race to the kitchen
fry up bacon, scramble eggs for a dozen
country relatives perched on davenports
like crows on power lines in November
I bound upstairs, bang the door to wake
seven teenaged girls who ought to eat
and though I bear heavy responsibilities
I skip weightless, stirring cautious smiles
from badgers baring teeth in a friendly way

Eduard Schmidt-Zorner
REPUBLIC OF IRELAND / GERMANY

Eduard is a translator and writer of poetry, haibun, haiku and short stories. He writes in four languages: English, French, Spanish and German, and holds workshops on Japanese and Chinese style poetry and prose, and experimental poetry. His work has been published in over 100 anthologies, literary journals and broadsheets worldwide including in the USA, UK, Ireland, Japan, Sweden, Italy, Bangladesh, India, France, Mauritius, Nigeria and Canada. His poems and haibun have been published in Romanian and Russian language. Born in Germany and lives in County Kerry for more than 25 years, Eduard ia a member of four writer groups in Ireland, and is a proud Irish citizen.
E: EadbhardMcGowan@gmx.com

FATHER FROST

Far in the taiga
is the Christmas Village,
behind the tundra
deep in the Siberian winter
at the polar circle,
behind the mountains,
where Christmas spirit prevails
with snow and icy temperatures
throughout the year
and you can sit by the warm fire
and drink punch or vodka
or *Glögg*.
in the company of Grandfather Frost,
who invites everyone to a drink
under the northern lights,
where the stars blink
under the green veil of the *aurora borealis*.

No matter where you come from,
you are most welcome:
the Irish drink their hot whiskey,
the Germans their Grog,
the Scandinavians *Glögg*, mulled wine
or rum with sugar - with water (but not necessarily)
The Russians drink hot tea from the samovar
and also hundred gram vodka
with Black sea caviar.

The reindeer and the moose
look over the fence
and the reindeer herder takes a snooze
and the hare in the wide forest
and the bear and wolves
listen to the songs
and the Advent's poem's rhyme
of the people at this cosy time.

All wait for Grandfather Frost
to return from his work,
he has received over two million letters
with wish lists from children
all over the world,

he is in the company of his granddaughter
and helper *Snegurotchka*
who wears a silver-blue coat
and a snowflake-like crown.

Here he is,
he comes in a snowstorm
and rides a troika.
He has a long white beard,
wears a red coat,
and felt boots on his feet.

"Ho ho ho", he shouts
and waves with his staff,
throws bags of presents into the snow.
We open the parcels:
There are 'Happiness' and 'Health',
There are 'Friendship' and 'Fellowship'
and 'Goodwill' and 'Peace',
And the biggest one
A gift for mankind:
'Love and Empathy'...

Ndaba Sibanda
ZIMBABWE / ETHIOPIA

Originally from Bulawayo, Zimbabwe but now living in Addis Ababa, Ethiopia, Ndaba is the author of *Notes, Themes, Things And Other Things, The Gushungo Way, Sleeping Rivers, Love O'clock, The Dead Must Be Sobbing, Football of Fools, Cutting-edge Cache, Of the Saliva and the Tongue, When Inspiration Sings In Silence, The Way Forward, Sometimes Seasons Come With Unseasonal Harvests, As If They Minded:The Loudness Of Whispers, This Cannot Be Happening :Speaking Truth To Power, The Dangers Of Child Marriages:Billions Of Dollars Lost In Earnings And Human Capital, The Ndaba Jamela and Collections* and *Poetry Pharmacy*. Ndaba's work has received Pushcart Prize and Best of the Net nominations. Some of his work has been translated into Serbian.
E: loveoclockn@gmail.com

WHEN THE SUN SMILED ON FUN

I drifted into childhood memories
I visualised loaves of bread, lorries

of it too. Villagers embraced
it in their way. It paced

into their lives. A holiday.
Christmas Day. What a day.

The beauty of its traditions,
the village ignited into celebrations.

Supersonic radios roared into the night,
the partying pack was my chief delight.

New clothes for kids. Wasn't that special?
New! Forget about 'debt' or 'commercial'.

Francis H. Powell
ENGLAND

Francis is a poet and writer. His anthology of short stories called *Flight of Destiny* was published in 2015 by Savant Publishing, and his second book *Adventures of Death, Reincarnation and Annihilation* was published by Beacon Publishing in 2019. At present Francis is putting together a book of short stories, poems and illustrations for the charity Marie Curie Nurses, which will be published winter 2020.
E: powellfrancisvid@gmail.com
W: www.francishpowellauthor.weebly.com
FB: @togetherbehindfourwalls

ANOTHER CHRISTMAS

I woke up with a large sock filled
with small toys and at the bottom an orange
Perhaps still believing in Santa Clause
or some such tomfoolery
It was a woolly sock, one of my fathers
He wore them while shooting pheasants
But he never was a good shot, or so I'm told
Christmas,
Oh all those family arguments
fixed in the memory
sitting round the table
overeating
Fighting with a chunk of turkey
some over cooked sprouts
and incinerated roast potatoes
Oh what joy!
A Christmas pudding filled
with six pences, my Mother had hidden
wrapped in baking paper
and thankfully not swallowed.
Surrounded by dates, tangerines and other delights
and crackers to be pulled
Then
Sat on a sofa
As the Queen solemnly made her annual speech
telling the nation, how to live good lives
and pointing out great things that have been achieved
in all her far off minions
There is a James Bond film to watch
007 adds some energy to Christmas Day
battling with outrageous fiends
dodging bullets while seducing women
with his flagrant charm
The Christmas cake, to fill the belly furthermore
Mince pies to munch, with dinner still to come
despite walking about bloated
There's the dogs to walk
Christmas wrapping paper binned or placed in the a roaring fire
Once again another Christmas is over.

Kathryn Sadakierski
USA

Kathryn is an American writer from Massachusetts whose work has appeared in *Capsule Stories, Critical Read, Halfway Down the Stairs, Literature Today, NewPages Blog, Northern New England Review, Origami Poems Project, seashores: an international journal to share the spirit of haiku, Snapdragon: A Journal of Art and Healing, Yellow Arrow Journal*, and elsewhere. She holds a B.A. from Bay Path University, and is currently pursuing her master's degree.
E: sadski7@gmail.com

CHRISTMAS LIGHTS

Evergreen boughs still wreath
Across the proud facades
Of clapboard and brick,
Candles like children
Watching for the first snowflakes
From each window,
Where light creates a soft froth,
Warm countenances
On the panes.

Strings of Christmas bulbs,
Crowning the trees,
In all their regal elegance,
Tiered resplendence,
Glitter as brightly as ever,
Like firecrackers,
Outlining the satin dress of night
In silver beads,
Trails of stars,
Intertwined like cursive letters,
Eternal words
Striking wonder into our hearts
That never are too full
For glimmers of joy,
Of hope,
Never too old
For childlike awe
Of all that still shines
With the love that Christmas instils.

Christmas traditions live on
In us,
And no amount of change
Can cause the magic
To fade.

FUSEE

the holidays
vary by tradition,
unique expression,
but no matter the circumstances
we find ourselves in,
they are characterized
by togetherness.

in quarantine,
there was time
to notice,
to simply be,
and so it became apparent
that each day can be made
special

not based on what we do,
or the things we collect,
but because of who we are with,
the laughs we share,
tears we help each other dry,
parting the clouds
to bring back the sun.

there was no need
to wait for one day
in November, or December,
to say what we are thankful for,
or to give gifts
of hope, peace, and joy.

they say that this season
will be different,
but when we are together,
in heart or home,
the core spirit of the holidays,
the reason,
persists,

the light still burning,
no matter the headwinds,
so we know that

under the outward wrappings,
the present
is still here,
with us.

Utpal Chakraborty
INDIA

A teacher of English literature, translator, writer, critic and bilingual poet Utpal is an Indian poet, residing in Kolkata. He is a regular contributor to leading Bengali and English magazines. His Concept, containing critical appreciations of prose and poetry, and his eight books based on grammar, rhetoric, prosody and writing skill released by the Kolkata based Nabodaya Publications, have been well received by the teachers and the taught alike. Charaborty's *@Uranta Dolphin*, an acclaimed collection of fifty five Bengali poems was published by Signet Press in 2018. He has translated Bitan Chakraborty's critically acclaimed collection of Bengali short stories, under the title *The Mark* (Shambhabi Imprint, 2020). His book of English poetry *@kirigami* recently published by @Hawakal, has had rave reviews by reputed poets and critics. His poem *@Eka Nou Jeno (Don't Think You are Alone)* written during the pandemic, has been widely appreciated and critiqued in English and Bengali newspapers. Several of his poems recited by the celebrated artists of Bengal have found home on *@Mango&Magenta* YouTube Channel.
E: sujato.uc@rediffmail.com

MONOCHROME

Snow precipitates the night
giving way to its cohort.
Mistletoe and cherries thread the dots.
Air's ablaze with chandeliers.
Children nod to the beats of cosy carols.
Reindeer gallop near.
A greying hair gets dolled up in fir, ever green.
Stockings get swollen with candied dreams.

A fairy tale hints at monochromes.

REVELATION

When the world is abuzz with
the songs of the choir,
when glare thickens the misty screen,
and the interiors pattern
Christmas hangings,

some tech-savvy children who love
chocolates with logic slip through
the net of chimneys and socks.
They hack the sack of the green old man.
A sea of emerald tears spills the beans.
The homeless billionaire in firs
collects the griefs through the years.
Blending them with his own
he makes an industry of chocolates and love.
Altruism returned ten times.

25 DECEMBER

As the quicksilver slides further,
Kolkata chills out on skewers,
north wind adding to the cheers
in saloons and pubs.

Angels and stars mount the tinsel firs.
Street artistes belt out Christmas tunes.
Every crossing is decked with Santa Caps.
Midnight city challenges the winter solstice.
Chocolates today will serve slums a filling meal.
A dreamy eye in the suburb looks into the biting air
for an epiphany.

His octogenarian grandfather
flashes his wisdom on a home succulent.
A stone decor gets live opening an evergreen leaf.
I see Hyperboreans spreading everywhere.

LindaAnn LoSchiavo
USA

LindaAnn is a dramatist, writer, and poet. Her poetry collections *Conflicted Excitement* (Red Wolf Editions, 2018), *Concupiscent Consumption* (Red Ferret Press, 2020), and Elgin Award nominee *A Route Obscure and Lonely* (Wapshott Press, 2020) along with her collaborative book on prejudice (Macmillan in the USA, Aracne Editions in Italy) are her latest titles. A member of The Dramatists Guild and SFPA, she was recently Poetry Superhighway's "Poet of the Week."
Twitter: @Mae_Westside

THE LEGEND OF LA BEFANA

Needing directions, the three wise men knocked.
Then La Befana welcomes them, prepares
Delicious food for high-born guests, asks where
They're headed with expensive gifts. They talked
About a star, a newborn. She was shocked.
Who is he? *"A Messiah! The night sky flares*
To guide us, carrying gold, precious wares.
Come with us!" they said. But Befana balked.

Alone she gets involved with housework but,
Soon realizing her mistake, she runs
Outside. Their holy quest has her beguiled.
Where's Bethlehem? Which road is the shortcut?
Too late! Ashamed, a new solution comes.
Each Christmas she'll go searching for this child.

Dr. Archana Bahadur Zutshi
INDIA

Archana has a Ph.D in English Poetry, and is based at Lucknow, India. She is widely published and acclaimed as a poet and author, and has two volumes of poetry titled: *Poetic Candour* and *The Speaking Muse*. Her poems have been published in national and international anthologies and journals including *All Poetry, United by Ink, Spillwords, Confluence, Setu, The Bilingual Journal, The Madras Courier, MirrorSpeak, Duatrope Poetry Blog* and others, and her poetry was featured by *Culturium* (March 18, 2019) on the occasion of Women's Day and Poetry Day. She is a translator of both poetry and prose from Hindi to English, and her essays in criticism are published as chapters in literary texts. Archana has won appreciation and commendable mentions in contests conducted by *United by Ink, POEMarium, Asian Literary Society, On Fire Cultural Movement* and *My Words: A Renaissance.*
E: zutshiarchana@gmail.com
FB: @zutshiarchana
Instagram: @zutshiarchana
Twitter: @ArchanaBahadurZ
YouTube: @ZutshiA

CHRISTMAS TIME

Christmas is a rhythmic beat of winters.
Faith and hope in crisis must glimmer
Just like the star that over Bethlehem did shimmer.
The travesty of Covid challenges
Power, pelf and position anon
Circuit of man's complacence undone

I was despairing the falling roof
He gave me the wonder of His benediction.
Then my eyes beheld a smooth transition.

Christmas is the joy of giving, Never revel in receiving!
The winter chill seems to thrive, But the bonfire radiates soothing comfort.
Jubilant carols bind us through lands distant.
Unkept promises, treacherous times
Decode verily the ambush of the faithless.
Christ is the newborn hope of the world in viral throes.
Watch, stay calm in quarantine,
The healed man cannot repudiate Nature
A blasphemy for the millennial sustenance!

Hail the Healer, hail the nativity.
Assimilate the Christmas fervour,
Sing the song of trust and faith,
Suffusing joy fathomed at the farthest hearth.

Mantz Yorke
ENGLAND

Mantz is a former science teacher and researcher living in Manchester, England. His poems have appeared in a number of print magazines, anthologies and e-magazines in the UK, Ireland, Israel, Canada, the US, Australia and Hong Kong. His collection *Voyager* is published by Dempsey & Windle.
E: mantzyorke@mantzyorke.plus.com

CHRISTMAS SCENE

The three kings, dressed opulently
in curtains and aluminium foil,
knelt reverently before the manger's haloed doll
to lay down the traditional gifts
of myrrh, frankincense and gold,
the final tableau in the cold church.

We sang 'We three kings'
(fortissimo, but rather tunelessly),
then shook the vicar's hand
before trudging back along the snow-packed lane
with rime glistening on the trees
and blue shadows stretching across the fields.

This Christmas snow, portrayed on millions of cards,
led us to forget the forecast warming:
we were surprised, next morning,
by the tarmac's re-emergence
and the rime-crystal lying like wormcasts
on grubby melting snow.

Mark Andrew Heathcote
ENGLAND

Mark is from Manchester. His poetry has been published in many journals, magazines and anthologies worldwide, and is the author of *In Perpetuity* and *Back on Earth,* two books of poems published by a CTU publishing group ~ Creative Talents Unleashed. Mark is adult learning difficulties support worker, who began writing poetry at an early age at school.
E: mrkheathcote@yahoo.co.uk

THE PIPES OF CHRISTMAS PAST

The thistle-down rises
On the north winds blast
Old Scotland calls the pipes
The pipes of Christmas past

Snow on the snow fleeced-land
Where the grouse run rich
With the golden-hare
Beyond the fox's caverns lair

Beyond the Mull of Kintyre
Beyond the Irish Sea
The pagan wood and the pagan tree
Is the heart world of Christianity?

THE SMOKING BISHOP

Made with Seville oranges stuck with cloves
and slowly roasted drank and eaten with loaves
grate in some nutmeg with a race of ginger
the rind of a lemon, it's heavenly, winter.
A famous drink, known as the Smoking Bishop,
it was once a popular, winter ticket.
In Victorian England at Christmas time
but nowadays it's-simply called Mulled wine.

Served in bowls, shaped headgear resembling
a Bishops Mitre, warm and welcoming
of course, recipes have now changed over time.
They'd use oranges a taste of Clementine.
It was then served in, medieval guildhalls,
universities it's had lots of spin-offs
it appears in Dickens' A Christmas Carol
it was made with claret, drank by the barrel.

Lou Faber
USA

Lou resides in Port St. Lucie, Florida. His work has previously appeared in *The Poet, Atlanta Review, Arena Magazine* (Australia), *Exquisite Corpse, Rattle, Eureka Literary Magazine, Borderlands:* the *Texas Poetry Review, Midnight Mind, Pearl, Midstream, European Judaism, Greens Magazine, The Amethyst Review, Afterthoughts, The South Carolina Review* and *Worcester Review*, and in small journals in India, Pakistan, China and Japan, among many others. Lou has also been nominated for a Pushcart Prize.
E: lfaberfl@outlook.com
W: www.anoldwriter.com
W: www.bird-of-the-day.com

ON THIS DAY

It is December, and in this
part of Florida that simply means
that a morning jacket is advised,
and rain comes as a bit of a surprise.

A neighbour was surprised to be told
that they decorated like a Northerner,
but assumed that it was a bit of a dig,
though they thought the inflatable snowman
and reindeer captured the season's spirit.

We laugh at the red hat wearing
flamingo's and the Christmas alligators,
the lighted palm trees seem appropriate
and snowflakes, even lit ones, know
better than to appear, for the mocking
of ibis and egrets can be unmerciful.

So we'll settle for our odd little tree
with its lifetime of ornaments, each
carrying with it the spirit of a day
when we ought to ask ourselves what
we can do to prepare the world
for the generations we hope will follow.

AN AWAKENING

Take one part
Grand Marnier, one
Frangelico, a short cup
of coffee, whipped cream
only if you wish,
curl on the sofa
with your life's
greatest love
and your first
real, truly your
first Christmas Eve
makes you wonder
why you waited
so long.

Dr. Eftichia Kapardeli
GREECE

Eftichia has a Doctorate from Arts and Culture World Academy. Born in Athens and lives in Patras, she writes poetry, stories, short stories, xai-kou, essays and novels. She studied journalism at AKEM (Athenian Training Centre), University of Cyprus in Greek culture. She has contributed to a number of international poetry collections and has won many awards in both national and international competitions. Eftichia is also a member of the IWA and The World Poets Society.
E: kapardeli@gmail.com
FB: @kapardeli.eftichia

CHRISTMAS

White flakes
fall to the ground
decorate children's heads
set in a sweet voice
and silver triangles
in their icy hands
the carols sing

Christmas and the
little Christ is born
Good day lords...
and if it is your definition...
Christ the divine birth
to say in your mansion

children's chants
Happy birthday and wishes
the little Christ
please
who is born tonight

to the poor children who are in pain
who do not have mom and dad
bread and sweets
who do not have toys
to bring them
many gifts
and a warm hug
sweets to love them

David A Banks
ENGLAND

David escaped from the confines of academic writing and now roams the fresh pastures of poetry and theatre, where he encounters far less bull. He regularly earwigs on conversations in a number of café haunts under the guise of 'research'. When not reading or writing, he has been known to make wooden dolls' houses, manufacture interesting pieces of firewood on a lathe, or spend many hours in the garden planning what he might do next time the weather conditions are absolutely perfect. He lives by the wise words of a respected friend who advised that most work activities should be given 'a good coat of looking-at' before commencing.
E: traveldab@gmail.com

CHRISTMAS TREE JOURNAL

Time to resurrect Christmas once again
To exhume the shrouded body of the tree
And the attic-dusted bauble box.

As each piece is carefully unwrapped
We make our annual journey down memory lane,
Recalling people and places in times gone by.

Look ... Poland, and Finland - do you remember?
And here's Moscow and, oh, where was this?
Yes, yes, that's right, how could I forget.

This one hung on my grandparents tree.
This one belonged to my parents.
This one was made by a long-departed friend.

Glass and plastic, wood and fabric,
Cheap and expensive, gaudy and tasteful,
Each carrying within it reminders of life's sadness and joys.

And when Christmas is over
Tree and baubles will once more be interred
Back in the attic, waiting to refresh us next year.

Martin Chrispine Juwa
MALAWI

Martin is a Secondary School teacher and lives in Lilongwe, Malawi. He loves to teach History, Life Skills and Social Studies. When he is not teaching, he reads and writes poetry, and composes music. Teaching is his passion, and he is happy to spend his days in the classroom. Martin believes that poetry gives people a platform to purge their innermost feelings, and that reading poems heals people from a variety of ailments. He is an advocate of social justice and morality through poetry and music. Some call him 'bleeding pen' because he is in many ways creative with pen and paper. Martin's articles and poetry are widely published in both local and international magazines, anthologies, journals and newspapers.
E: chrisjuwa@gmail.com

SMALL TOWN OF BETHLEHEM

In the small town of Bethlehem, joy ascended
Diving straight up like thin tendrils crawling up a stem
Swirling up, it sank its teeth in the narrow
Paths of the town.
Lodges were filled up with old timers and strangers
Who, abusing the worn-out pavements with heavy, tired feet
Clutched bits of air also.
Joseph and Mary bounced from corner to corner like light rays
Searching for lodging
And found none
But a manger
And the baby Jesus stirred for the first time
With a cry of a Mighty King...

Maliha Hassan
PAKISTAN

Maliha is an educationist from Pakistan. She has completed a Masters in English Literature and Linguistics, a Masters in TEFL (Teaching English as a Foreign Language), and has around 30 years teaching and administrative experience to her credit. Her poems have been published in various international anthologies, and is the author of the e-book *Thought Provoking Poems, Reflections of a Thoughtful Mind*. She exposes the harsh realities of society in a subtle manner. There is a touch of religious and didactic verses which appeals to young and old alike.
E: mlh.hassan@gmail.com

CELEBRATION

A yearly celebration, a day to rejoice,
Of limit of happiness can there be a choice?
Chanting happily Christmas carols,
Giving away from the decorated barrels.
Gifts wrapped in colourful paper,
Giving full credit to its maker.
Forgetting for once all strife and fear,
All niceties made with special care.
Turkeys roasted in mustard and pepper,
Speaks volumes of its skilful baker.
Served with jars of herbs and sauces,
Offered lavishly to elites, less masses.
New clothes, latest attire, the best of best,
Ready to be worn, furnished with a crest.
All set and offered for choices to be made,
Alterations and adjustments of any shade.

Men and women attending in pair,
Enhancing appearances in makeup layer.
Setting the tables with all sorts of gifts,
For friends, families even those with rifts.
Sparkling lights of various hue,
Enjoyed by all, their rightful due.
The city decorated like a pretty bride,
Street poles glittering on each side.
Sparkling lights of various hue,
Enjoyed by all, their rightful due.
Like stars descending on a starry night,
Spreading serenity with radiance bright.
The fairy-like ambience trying to withhold,
Permanent happiness on their threshold.
But what about the ones below the line?
Negating them of love is listed a crime.
Let's join hands with the ones deprived.
Lift the innocent souls who silently cried.
Little acts can bring happiness or smile.
Spirits will be lifted, at least for a while.
Greater the feeling, greater the care.
Let's lift up the desperate from fear.
A flavour of happiness they may enjoy,
To ask for help, they may be shy.
No diamond, expensive jewels nor gold,

All they want is your warm caring hold.
Love, warm hug and a smile to console,
Temporarily for the ones out on parole.
Opportunity we get this once a year,
In pretence of happiness our yearly care.

Donna Zephrine
USA

Donna was born in Harlem, New York and grew up in Bay Shore, Long island. She graduated from Columbia University School of Social Work in May 2017, and currently works for the New York State Office of Mental Health at Pilgrim Psychiatric Center Outpatient SOCR (State Operated Community Residence). She is a combat veteran who completed two tours in Iraq. She was on active duty army, stationed at Hunter Army Airfield 3rd infantry Division as a mechanic. Since returning home, Donna enjoys sharing her experiences and storytelling through writing. Donna's stories most recently have been published in *New York Times, On The Road, War and Battle, The Seasons, Qutub Minar Review, Bards Initiative, Radvocate, Oberon, Long Island Poetry Association* and *The Mighty*.
E: kauldonna@yahoo.com
FB: @donna.zephrine
Twitter: @dzephrine
Instagram: @donnazephrine
LinkenIn: @donna-zephrine-30300636

CHRISTMAS TRADITIONS IN WEST INDIES

It's the week before Christmas
time to get ready for the holiday.
Cleaning everything from top to bottom.
making sure the house is painted and
ready for Christmas decorations.
Red curtains were hung to every window
and all the bedding is changed as well.
Making the house look and smell like Christmas.

Baked ham, chicken and curry goat,
Sit in the centre of the Christmas table
Chalouh, macaroni cheese pie, corn on the cob,
candied yams and rice and peas
surround the steaming meats like Christmas decoration.
home-made bread, ginger beer, mauby, and sorrel
are all on the Christmas table too.

Christmas fruit cake also called black cake,
mostly made for Christmas
dark or white rum and wine,
raisins, prunes, currants, sugar and flour were
the major ingredients of the fruit cake
the fruit mix would be placed in a glass bottle, pale or bucket
to sit for months before the actual baking began.

Family coming from far and near. Bringing more food to share.
some family members would stay overnight
and have a good-by breakfast the next day
Happy, noisy children playing with new toys from under the tree
adults talking and laughing and reminiscing
of childhood past and new events to come up.

Alicja Maria Kuberska
POLAND

Alicja Maria is an award winning Polish poet, novelist, journalist and editor. She is a member of the Polish Writers Association in Warsaw, and IWA Bogdani, Albania. She is also a member of the directors' board of the Soflay Literature Foundation, Our Poetry Archive (India) and Cultural Ambassador for Poland (Inner Child Press, USA). Her poems have been published in numerous anthologies and magazines in Poland, Czech Republic, Slovakia, Hungary, Belgium, Bulgaria, Albania, Spain, the UK, Italy, the USA, Canada, Argentina, Chile, Peru, Israel, Turkey, India, Uzbekistan, South Korea, Taiwan, Australia, South Africa, Zambia, and Nigeria.
E: alicja107@vp.pl

EXPECTATION

Empty chair by the Christmas table.
Thousands of glittering flames
Dance on colourful ornaments.
The whole world trembles, it slowly rocks.
Green spruce smells like the woods.

Like Ariadne, I weave
Angel hair into memories and silence.
I return to happy hours,
To events that are now but dreams.
I listen to every murmur, rustle.
It seems, that at last I will hear
Familiar footsteps on the other side of the door.

CHRISTMAS SEASON

Light is born on the longest night.
Love and goodness show the way in the darkness,
A chance to break selfishness.

Time slows and strikes the hours reflectively,
Faces appear from the crowd,
It's possible to smile, say a few nice words.

Empathy and tenderness have a sweet taste,
Mercy generously bestows gifts,
Time for rebirth.

Lindsay Ronald
CANADA

Lindsay is an artist and writer who lives in London, Ontario. She has a deep affection for nature, which is a strong theme throughout her poetry. Through writing, she attempts to explore the beautiful and complex relationships between emotion and the natural environment. Lindsay has worked for several years as an Early Childhood Educator, and is grateful that her work with young children keeps her curious about the world around her.
E: lindsayronald@hotmail.com
W: www.versesinseason.com

CHRISTMAS TREE

The spirit of the season
Is a glowing altar,
In the corner
Of our living room.

A temple of folk art and fir
And fragrant body,
A tangible heart
Adorned.

June G Paul
USA

June is from the four-season State of Wisconsin who had a desire in grade school to influence people's lives through creative writing. And she has; most often through simply sharing her poems, reflections and stories. Her life as a student, and in her careers, took her through adventures in studying Psychology and Christianity, and earning a Master Degree in Religious Studies. Her career path has taken her through the food and financial industries, retail sales, direct sales, elderly care in activities and spiritual care, and substitute teachers' aide in the local school. While recovering from a serious illness, and at the encouragement of members in a local writing group, June began to write with more of an intent to publish. She enjoys encouraging other people, spending time with family and dabbling in creative arts. June is a member of Wisconsin Fellowship of Poets and participates regularly in an annual Art the Blooms program held at a local gallery. June is also a member of the Council of Wisconsin Writer's. She has self-published two books, *Praying our Way Through Stress* and *A Stable Birth*. She has poems published in the *Blue Heron Review, The Poet by Day, Grief Digest (Centering.org), HaikUniverse, Ekphrastic.net, Visual Verse* and an article on *TrishHopkinson.com*.
E: junegpaul@gmail.com

SANTA DREW NEAR

Not wanting to be a stranger,
Santa Claus came to the manger,
He drew very near,
to Jesus so dear,
and called Him his Lord and Saviour.

ON CHRISTMAS EVE

The children put milk, cookies, sausage and cheese
on plates near the tree for Santa to see.
Now that they're snuggling all warm
in their beds, the mice in the walls
aren't sleeping at all.
They're looking for holes
Through which they can crawl.

Keith Burton
USA

Born and raised in Europe and Asia to American parents, Keith went to university in the States and majored in psychology with a minor in English. Later, he became a musician and has written a number of songs. A significant influence in his life was attending British boarding school for second and third form, which gave him a lifelong admiration for English poets. The curriculum was rigorous however, he did meet Bob Dylan at Heathrow Airport when he was 13, so it was well worth it. He currently lives in San Diego, California where Christmas ornaments adorn palm trees.

E: keith1080@gmail.com

THE ANGELIC HOST

We waited for the moment of his birth, every angel in heaven in a grand circle in the sky.
When he arrived, we thundered our wings ringing stars like tiny bells.
From the oldest angel to the youngest cherub, we longed to see the child and archangels led the heavenly procession.
He was born at night and none recalled such beauty, onyx with a shine of moonlight.
We sang great hallelujahs, vast clouds of harmony bending air to glide music down to earth.
Shepherds descended hills under a smiling star while kings hurried their camels along.
And there he was, a child in a manger, a cherub leading the world to love!
Heaven and earth shared a greeting, and no angel had to work that night, so holy was the evening.

Gabriella Garofalo
ITALY

Born in Italy some decades ago, at age just six, Gabriella both fell in love with the English language and started writing poems in Italian She has contributed to a number of national and international magazines and anthologies, and is the author of *Lo sguardo di Orfeo, L'inverno di vetro, Di altre stelle polari, Casa di erba, Blue branches* and *A Blue Soul*.
E: grrz2001@yahoo.it

TO N, H, T - MY FIXED STARS

I know, I know, my angels, wise men,
My shepherds, my stars,
I know you're feeling bit weary,
Same old same old every year,
Hey presto, dash off to the manger,
Songs, lambs, gold, incense, myrrh,
Same old same old every year -
Now listen, just for once, just for a change,
Give the newborn something else,
Warn him the comet he beholds
Can't shelter from shadows,
Same shadows I met
When seething with anger at the worn green
From berries, or the stilted magenta
From wreaths on a tree, while people got
All kind'n' cosy, 'don't bother with trifles'
They went -
But where were stars, angels, and starlit skies
To warn me?
Tell him to slowly tiptoe
When heading for the living room,
Tell him to say no to berries, or trees,
But to grin at the white her soul met
When stroking the snow,
So to let stillness be a blessing
To her, the soul, and angels in a silent vault -
Minstrels, or songs, let him in the dark,
White only, that great silent white
Where prayers and tears,
Concerns and whatnot, told just for a kick,
Are taken for granted, where hopes and acceptance
Might even get life -
Then my kiddos, their un-fazed light
And you, God, in the light of your silence -
All white.

Wilda Morris
USA

Wilda lives in Bolingbrook, Illinois, with her husband of 57 years. She is Workshop Chair of Poets and Patrons of Chicago, past President of the Illinois State Poetry Society, and for many years attended the San Miguel Poetry Week in Mexico. She has published over 600 poems in anthologies, webzines, and print publications including *The Ocotillo Review, Pangolin Review, Poetry Sky, Whitefish Review, Quill & Parchment* (for which she was the featured poet in November 2020), and *Journal of Modern Poetry*. For three years she chaired the Stevens Poetry Manuscript Competition, and has won awards for formal and free verse and haiku, including the 2019 Founders' Award from the National Federation of State Poetry Societies in the U.S. Much of the work on her second poetry book *Pequod Poems: Gamming with Moby-Dick* (published in 2019), was written during a Writer's Residency on Martha's Vineyard. For 14 years, she has moderated a monthly poetry reading at Brewed Awakening Coffeeshop in Westmont, Illinois. A retired educator, Wilda has five children, fifteen grandchildren and seven great-grandchildren and is currently working on a book of poetry inspired by books and articles on scientific topics.
E: wem@ameritech.net
W: www.wildamorris.blogspot.com

THE SAME PAGEANT

Each year, the same pageant,
the same belted gowns
and glitter-glued wings,
the same tinfoil star.

Each year, different Joseph
leads a different Mary
to the cardboard stable
where she lays the same
baby Jesus on the straw
while children, some
the same, some different,
crawl in lamb costumes
toward the Holy Family,
led by bathrobed shepherds
carrying the same staffs.

Each year, my same eyes
watch, my same ears listen
to angel songs sung by small
voices, some the same,
some different, and my same
soul is stirred by unnamed
feelings, always serene,
always grateful.

CHRISTMAS GIFT FOR MOTHER

Grandmother let me cut
the coupon from her magazine,
provided the envelop,
three-cent stamp
and shiny dime.
But it was my small hands
which carefully taped
the coin to the coupon,
scrawled my name and address.
With my own tongue
I licked the stamp.
When the tiny sample
of Jergens' Lotion arrived,
I packaged it in Christmas wrap,
and love.

ROSCA DE REYES

Under a white cloth, yeast does its work
on the flour, sugar and eggs, causes them to rise,
conceal candied fruit and the petite plastic baby
as the ancient story says Joseph hid the infant
from the murderous hands of Herod.
This ring of sweet bread, crowns the celebration
of Three Kings Day, *Dia de los Reyes*.
The one who finds the babe in the risen loaf
is blessed, and bidden to the task of hospitality,
providing tamales for Candlemas.

Meanwhile, here in San Miguel de Allende,
children tie their wishes to balloons, send them
aloft, destined to be delivered to the *Los Reyes*
who arrive at dusk, all on horseback,
not Caspar's camel or Balthazar's elephant.
The faces of the three monarchs, beneath crowns
and turbans, show varied skin tones, dark
to light, as varied as the faces of expectant children
gathered to cheer them, to sit on their laps
and whisper secret hopes. Smiling parents
stand by, hoping to overhear the children's dreams
above the sounds of the band, the camera-bearing *touristas*,
the periodic peal of bells from La Parroquia,
and the long line of restless girls and boys
politely awaiting their turns.

Previously published in *Songs of Eretz Poetry Review* (Winter 2019).

Veda Varma
KINGDOM OF BAHRAIN / INDIA

Veda is a 14 year old Indian teenager living in the Kingdom of Bahrain. She is a poetry, guitar and drama enthusiast. Her talent and love for poetry came as a complete surprise when a school assignment pushed her to give poems a try. Writing has now become one of her greatest passions, and writes about topics that leave the reader puzzled and questioning themselves.
Instagram: @_houseofpoetry

AT A DISTANCE...

Underneath the glistening snow,
Hands filled with warm cocoa.
Festivities screaming delight,
Fairy lights illuminating the night.

From treats to rampaging streets,
The atmosphere loaded with love and joy.
The Christmas tree submerged in snow,
I pray for those feeling low.

I spot a feast, at the end of the street,
Gingerbread for the kids,
The babies fast asleep in their cribs!
The adults get roast chicken,
Those under the mistletoe, completely smitten!

At a distance, I see a young boy,
Covered in rags, fiddling with his broken toy.
It's Christmas Eve, why doesn't his face radiate joy?
That's right, he has nothing to enjoy.

Hunger struck, his family torn apart,
He survives with nothing more than a beating heart.
I walk up to him, hot cocoa in hand,
Realization hits me; he doesn't have the strength to stand.

I ask him if he'd like some cookies,
He answers, with a shivering sneeze.
'I-i can't afford o-one,'
'N-neither a cookie, nor a b-bun.'

Broken by those words,
I run up to the food stall,
Fill my hands with treats,
Offer to show him the well-lit streets.

Christmas, a magnificent time,
A time with love, a time with joy.
Give all the luxury of comfort,
Ensure no child remains consumed by the hurt.

Provide for the hungry,

No one shall be missed,
Turn those frowns upside down,
And you won't make Santa's naughty list!

Mary Anne Zammit
MALTA

Mary Anne is a graduate from the University of Malta in Social Work, in Probation Services, in Diplomatic Studies and in Masters in Probation and has also obtained a Diploma in Freelance and Feature Writing from the London School of Journalism. She is the author of four novels in Maltese and two in English. Some of Mary Anne's literary works and poetry have also been featured in international magazines and anthologies and set to music and performed during the Mdina Cathedral Art Biennale in Malta. Also, her artistic works have been exhibited in various collective exhibitions both locally and abroad.

E: mariefrances3@gmail.com

MY LITTLE XMAS TREE

My little Xmas tree.
Standing proudly, waiting in silence.
I like to hug you and put your branches around me.
Reds, golds, silver to warm my heart.

My little Xmas tree
You bring back memories of other Christmas.
And I travel back with the silence of the stars.

Tonight, my little Xmas tree
At the early hours.
Do not forget the children who cannot feel this silence of this special
night.
And cannot see the star.

My little Xmas tree be their star.

MEMORIES OF CHRISTMAS

This Christmas.
I will buy mince pies for when you come.
And we will sit under the tree and like a phoenix we fly.
Back to other Christmases.

When children walked around the streets in our town and carried
the small baby child Jesus.
They sang carols and made us dream of a new hope.

What about the midnight ceremony?
Half asleep we went to follow the young boy
reciting word by word, the story of the King of the Universe born
amongst mankind.
For you and me.
And then came the mince pies, hot and sweet.
Yes, again this this Christmas we dream again.
Smile my dear, seems we have survived the year.
And you are here.
With our mince pies and memories.

Ed Ruzicka
USA

Raised beside creeks and cornfields near Chicago, Ed lives with his wife, Renee, in Baton Rouge, LA. Ed's new release, *My Life in Cars*, addresses the uniquely American marriage between highways and freedom. His work has appeared in the *Atlanta Review, Rattle, Canary* and myriad literary journals and anthologies.
E: edzekezone@gmail.com

YULETIDE

I am baking pecans, fallen, filched
off dirt from beside ants and worms
while the sun speared branches, while mist
stewed late past dawn, while rain splintered
into yarrow and the clay dove cooed its clay coo.
You can taste the rich, solitude of these nuts,
slow-cured in hard and bitter shells.

I am baking them at 350 within a dark slosh
of molasses, egg, butter, sugar, vanilla, set down
into crusts I pulled from a freezer at the supermarket,
checked out and slotted into our own Frigidaire
Left the crust forgotten until now when it sends its
heated bloom belling out through every room.

Fills me with anticipation for tomorrow when,
among family I will savour a slice toward the end
of the day when we are all punchy and bloto and ready
to totter off to our individual cars, down our chosen highways,
glide under tree branches that darken toward winter,
swollen and numb with a mammalian blood murmur
of content. Given up, each in our separate conveyances,
to a noiseless almost inert psalm of deep gratitude.

END